Learning ECMAScript 6

Learn all the new ES6 features and be among the most prominent JavaScript developers who can write efficient JS programs as per the latest standards!

Narayan Prusty

BIRMINGHAM - MUMBAI

Learning ECMAScript 6

Copyright © 2015 Packt Publishing

All rights reserved. No part of this book may be reproduced, stored in a retrieval system, or transmitted in any form or by any means, without the prior written permission of the publisher, except in the case of brief quotations embedded in critical articles or reviews.

Every effort has been made in the preparation of this book to ensure the accuracy of the information presented. However, the information contained in this book is sold without warranty, either express or implied. Neither the author nor Packt Publishing, and its dealers and distributors will be held liable for any damages caused or alleged to be caused directly or indirectly by this book.

Packt Publishing has endeavored to provide trademark information about all of the companies and products mentioned in this book by the appropriate use of capitals. However, Packt Publishing cannot guarantee the accuracy of this information.

First published: August 2015

Production reference: 1250815

Published by Packt Publishing Ltd.
Livery Place
35 Livery Street
Birmingham B3 2PB, UK.

ISBN 978-1-78588-444-3

www.packtpub.com

Credits

Author
Narayan Prusty

Reviewers
Andrea Chiarelli
Philippe Renevier Gonin
Domenico Luciani
Mihir Mone
Takeharu Oshida
Juri Strumpflohner

Commissioning Editor
Veena Pagare

Acquisition Editor
Aaron Lazar

Content Development Editor
Shweta Pant

Technical Editor
Rohith Rajan

Copy Editor
Yesha Gangani

Project Coordinator
Shipra Chawhan

Proofreader
Safis Editing

Indexer
Tejal Soni

Production Coordinator
Manu Joseph

Cover Work
Manu Joseph

Foreword

There is no better time than now to be working with JavaScript. Over the last few years, we've seen JavaScript go from being the language no one really wanted to touch to being the language that everyone can't wait to get their hands on. Large, complicated applications are being built everyday in browsers and are exercising and pushing JavaScript further than it has ever been pushed before. Frameworks and entirely new approaches to application design have spawned to meet the demands of this new world of client-side development, and the community has rallied around them.

With ECMAScript 2015, or ES6 as it's commonly known, we finally have the language to match our lofty ambitions. We've gained large, much needed functionalities, such as Promises, and a module system that is native to the language; we've also gained smaller, more subtle additions that make day-to-day development more enjoyable. Get familiar with object destructuring, and you'll wonder how you ever wrote JavaScript without it; use an arrow function for the first time, and you'll never want to type "function" again. Avoid the complications of function scope and leaky variables with "let", and you'll spend less time bashing your head against the desk.

Not only is ES6 a great language and an incredible upgrade on ES5, but the hard work of many members of the community also means that you can use it today and not have to wait for complete implementations in browsers. Tools exist to let you convert your ES6 code into ES5 compliant code, meaning the future's now, not 5 years down the line, as it so often is with JavaScript.

This book will guide you through a selection of the most useful additions to JavaScript and bring you up to the speed with the current functionality available to you. You'll learn how building modular applications is much easier with ES6's native module system and how your code can become cleaner, more succinct, and more enjoyable to work with. Learning this new standard is a daunting task for any developer, and I'm delighted to contribute a foreword toward a book that will make this task much less daunting.

This brave new world of JavaScript, client-side applications, frameworks, and more is being powered by ES6, and this book will help you take your first steps toward it. I hope you end this book as excited as I am.

Jack Franklin
JavaScript Developer at GoCardless
`@Jack_Franklin`
`http://www.jackfranklin.co.uk`

About the Author

Narayan Prusty is a web and mobile app developer. He specializes in WordPress, HTML5, JavaScript, PHP, Solr, and Cordova. He has been learning and building applications using these technologies for many years.

He is the founder of QScutter.com, which provides courses on various application development topics and has more than 10,000 subscribers worldwide. His personal blog, `http://www.QNimate.com`, is among the top Intel XDK and WordPress blogs. He also works as a consultant and freelance developer for many companies worldwide.

Visit him online at `http://www.twitter.com/narayanprusty`.

> Thanks first and foremost to the web community. Without their combined brilliance and generosity in documenting and sharing solutions, I wouldn't have been able to write this book. Finally, thanks to my family for being so supportive.

About the Reviewers

Andrea Chiarelli has over 20 years of experience as a software engineer and technical writer. In his professional career, he has used various technologies for the projects he has been involved in, from C# to JavaScript, ASP.NET to AngularJS, and REST to PhoneGap/Cordova.

He has contributed to many online and offline magazines, such as *Computer Programming* and *ASP Today*, and was a coauthor of a few books published by Wrox Press.

Currently, he is a senior software engineer at the Italian office of Apparound Inc., a mobile software company founded in the heart of Silicon Valley, and he is a regular contributor to HTML.it, an Italian online magazine focused on web technologies.

Philippe Renevier Gonin has been an assistant professor at the University of Nice Sophia Antipolis, France, since 2005. He teaches web technologies, software engineering (architecture and development), and HCI (Human Computer Interaction). From a research perspective, Philippe works on connections between user-centered design (for example, users and tasks models) and software engineering (for example, component architecture and UI development). In his projects, he often develops software and tools in Javascript, HMTL, CSS, and Java (Android).

Domenico Luciani is a 22-year-old passionate programmer. He is currently working as a software engineer for some companies and is pursuing a degree in computer science at The University of Palermo.

He is a computer vision enthusiast. He loves computer security and often pen-tests too; he takes part in bounty programs for many companies. He has worked on many technologies in the past, such as MongoDB, Node.js, PHP, PostgreSQL, and C.

He creates Node.js modules, which are published on the NPM website. He has collaborated as a reviewer and is currently learning GoLang just for fun.

He is also a part of the Maker community and likes working on his Raspberry Pi. He loves writing code using vim and managing it with Git. He also writes tests and collaborates on open source projects across the Web.

In his spare time, he is a runner and loves parkour. You can find more information about him at `http://www.dlion.it`.

Mihir Mone is a postgraduate from Monash University, Australia. Although he did his post graduation in network computing, these days, he mainly is into web and mobile development. After spending some time fiddling around with routers and switches, he quickly decided to build upon his passion for web development—not design, but development. Building web systems and applications rather than websites with all their fancy Flash animations was something that was very interesting and alluring to him. He even returned to his alma mater to teach web development in order to give back what he had learned.

Now, he works for a small software/engineering house in Melbourne, doing web development and prototyping exciting new ideas in the field of data visualization and UX domains.

He is also a big JavaScript fan and has previously reviewed a few books on jQuery and JavaScript. He is a Linux enthusiast and a big proponent of the OSS movement. He believes that software should always be free to actualize its true potential.

A true geek at heart, he spends some of his leisure time writing code in the hope that it may be helpful to the masses. You can find more information on him at `http://mihirmone.apphb.com`.

Takeharu Oshida (https://github.com/georgeOsdDev) works at a small start-up called Mobilus (http://mobilus.co.jp/). Mobilus provides a real-time communication platform and an SDK called Konnect.

As a JavaScript engineer, he designs JavaScript APIs, and creates React.JS-based web applications with ES6.

He is also a member of the Xitrum web framework project (http://xitrum-framework.github.io/). As a part of this project, he is learning the functional programming style of Scala by either creating sample applications or translating documents.

He has been a reviewer on *Learning Behavior-driven Development Javascript*, published by *Packt Publishing*.

Juri Strumpflohner is a passionate developer who loves to code, follow the latest trends on web development, and share his findings with others. He has been working as a coding architect and technical lead for an e-government company, where he is responsible for coaching developers, innovating, and making sure that the software meets the desired quality.

In his free time, he contributes to open source projects, does book reviews (like this one), tweets (@juristr), and writes about the latest web development tech news on his blog at http://juristr.com. Currently, he's particularly interested in ES 2015 (ES6), AngularJS, React, Babel, and all the hot stuff that comes with modern web development.

When not coding, Juri is either training or teaching Yoseikan Budo, a martial art where he currently has a 2nd DAN black belt. Follow him on twitter (@juristr) on the Web, or visit his blog at http://juristr.com to catch up with him.

www.PacktPub.com

Support files, eBooks, discount offers, and more

For support files and downloads related to your book, please visit www.PacktPub.com.

Did you know that Packt offers eBook versions of every book published, with PDF and ePub files available? You can upgrade to the eBook version at www.PacktPub.com and as a print book customer, you are entitled to a discount on the eBook copy. Get in touch with us at service@packtpub.com for more details.

At www.PacktPub.com, you can also read a collection of free technical articles, sign up for a range of free newsletters and receive exclusive discounts and offers on Packt books and eBooks.

https://www2.packtpub.com/books/subscription/packtlib

Do you need instant solutions to your IT questions? PacktLib is Packt's online digital book library. Here, you can search, access, and read Packt's entire library of books.

Why subscribe?

- Fully searchable across every book published by Packt
- Copy and paste, print, and bookmark content
- On demand and accessible via a web browser

Free access for Packt account holders

If you have an account with Packt at www.PacktPub.com, you can use this to access PacktLib today and view 9 entirely free books. Simply use your login credentials for immediate access.

Table of Contents

Preface vii
Chapter 1: Playing with Syntax 1
  The let keyword 1
    Declaring function scoped variables 2
    Declaring block scoped variables 3
    Re-declaring variables 4
  The const keyword 6
    The scope of constant variables 7
    Referencing the objects using constant variables 7
  Default parameter values 8
  The spread operator 9
    Other usages of the spread operator 11
      Making array values a part of another array 11
      Pushing the values of an array into another array 11
    Spreading multiple arrays 12
  The rest parameter 13
  The destructuring assignment 14
    The array destructuring assignment 14
      Ignoring values 15
      Using the rest operator in the array destructuring assignment 15
      Default values for variables 16
      Nested array destructuring 17
      Using the destructuring assignment as a parameter 17
    The object destructuring assignment 17
      Default values for the variables 18
      Destructuring computed property names 19
      Destructuring nested objects 19
      Using the object destructuring assignment as a parameter 19

The arrow functions	**19**
The value of "this" in an arrow function	20
Other differences between the arrow and traditional functions	22
The enhanced object literals	**22**
Defining properties	22
Defining methods	23
The computed property names	23
Summary	**24**
Chapter 2: Knowing Your Library	**25**
Working with numbers	**25**
The binary notation	26
The octal notation	26
The Number.isInteger(number) method	27
The Number.isNaN(value) method	28
The Number.isFinite(number) method	29
The Number.isSafeInteger(number) method	30
The Number.EPSILON property	30
Doing Math	**31**
Trigonometry related operations	32
Arithmetic related operations	32
Miscellaneous methods	33
The Math.imul(number1, number2) function	33
The Math.clz32(number) function	33
The Math.sign(number) function	34
The Math.trunc(number) function	34
The Math.fround(number) function	34
Working with strings	**35**
Escaping larger code points	36
The codePointAt(index) method	36
The String.fromCodePoint(number1, ..., number 2) method	36
The repeat(count) method	37
The includes(string, index) method	37
The startsWith(string, index) method	37
The endsWith(string, index) function	38
Normalization	38
A case study	38
Template strings	40
Expressions	40
Multiline strings	42
Raw strings	43

Arrays	**44**
The Array.from(iterable, mapFunc, this) method	44
The Array.of(values…) method	44
The fill(value, startIndex, endIndex) method	45
The find(testingFunc, this) method	46
The findIndex(testingFunc, this) method	47
The copyWithin(targetIndex, startIndex, endIndex) function	47
The entries(), keys(), and values() method	48
Collections	**49**
Array buffers	49
Typed arrays	51
Set	52
WeakSet	53
Map	54
WeakMap	55
Object	**56**
The __proto__ property	56
The Object.is(value1, value2) method	56
The Object.setPrototypeOf(object, prototype) method	57
The Object.assign(targetObj, sourceObjs…) method	57
Summary	**58**
Chapter 3: Using Iterators	**59**
The ES6 symbols	59
The "typeof" operator	60
The "new" operator	60
Using symbols as property keys	61
The Object.getOwnPropertySymbols() method	62
The Symbol.for(string) method	62
The well-known symbols	63
The iteration protocols	**64**
The iterator protocol	64
The iterable protocol	65
Generators	**66**
The return(value) method	68
The throw(exception) method	69
The "yield*" keyword	70
The "for…of" loop	**71**
The tail call optimization	**72**
Converting the non-tail calls into the tail calls	73
Summary	**74**

Table of Contents

Chapter 4: Asynchronous Programming — 75
The JavaScript execution model — 76
Writing asynchronous code — 76
The asynchronous code involving events — 77
The asynchronous code involving callbacks — 80
Promises to the rescue — 82
The Promise constructor — 83
The fulfillment value — 84
The then(onFulfilled, onRejected) method — 85
The catch(onRejected) method — 91
The Promise.resolve(value) method — 94
The Promise.reject(value) method — 94
The Promise.all(iterable) method — 95
The Promise.race(iterable) method — 96
The JavaScript APIs based on Promises — 97
The Battery Status API — 97
The Web Cryptography API — 98
Summary — 99

Chapter 5: Implementing the Reflect API — 101
The Reflect object — 101
The Reflect.apply(function, this, args) method — 102
The Reflect.construct(constructor, args, prototype) method — 102
The Reflect.defineProperty(object, property, descriptor) method — 103
Understanding the data properties and accessor properties — 104
The Reflect.deleteProperty(object, property) method — 106
The Reflect.enumerate(object) method — 107
The Reflect.get(object, property, this) method — 107
The Reflect.set(object, property, value, this) method — 108
The Reflect.getOwnPropertyDescriptor(object, property) method — 109
The Reflect.getPrototypeOf(object) method — 109
The Reflect.setPrototypeOf(object, prototype) method — 110
The Reflect.has(object, property) method — 110
The Reflect.isExtensible(object) method — 111
The Reflect.preventExtensions(object) method — 111
The Reflect.ownKeys(object) method — 112
Summary — 112

Chapter 6: Using Proxies — 113
Proxies in a nutshell — 113
Terminology — 114
The Proxy API — 114
Traps — 115
The get(target, property, receiver) method — 115
The set(target, property, value, receiver) method — 118
The has(target, property) method — 118
The isExtensible(target) method — 119
The getPrototypeOf(target) method — 120
The setPrototypeOf(target, prototype) method — 120
The preventExtensions(target) method — 121
The getOwnPropertyDescriptor(target, property) method — 122
The defineProperty(target, property, descriptor) method — 123
The deleteProperty(target, property) method — 124
The enumerate(target) method — 124
The ownKeys(target) method — 125
The apply(target, thisValue, arguments) method — 127
The construct(target, arguments) method — 128
The Proxy.revocable(target, handler) method — 128
Use Case — 129
The uses of proxies — 129
Summary — 130

Chapter 7: Walking You Through Classes — 131
Understanding the Object-oriented JavaScript — 131
The JavaScript data types — 132
Creating objects — 132
Understanding inheritance — 133
The constructors of primitive data types — 137
Using classes — 139
Defining a class — 139
The class declaration — 139
The class expression — 141
The prototype methods — 141
The get and set methods — 143
The generator method — 144
The static methods — 145
Implementing inheritance in classes — 146
The computed method names — 148
The attributes of properties — 149
Classes are not hoisted! — 149

Overriding the result of the constructor method	150
The "Symbol.species" static accessor property	150
The "new.target" implicit parameter	152
Using "super" in the object literals	**153**
Summary	**154**
Chapter 8: Modular Programming	**155**
The JavaScript modules in a nutshell	**155**
Implementing modules – the old way	**156**
The Immediately-Invoked Function Expression	156
Asynchronous Module Definition	158
CommonJS	159
Universal Module Definition	160
Implementing modules – the new way	**161**
Creating the ES6 modules	161
Importing the ES6 modules	162
The module loader	164
Using modules in browsers	164
Using modules in the eval() function	165
The default exports versus the named exports	165
Diving into an example	165
Summary	**167**
Index	**169**

Preface

ECMAScript is a scripting language standardized by Ecma International in the ECMA-262 specification and ISO/IEC 16262. Scripting languages such as JavaScript, JScript and ActionScript are supersets of ECMAScript. Although JavaScript, JScript, and ActionScript have more capabilities than ECMAScript, by defining more objects and methods, the core features of these languages are the same as ECMAScript.

ECMAScript 6 is the sixth version and the seventh edition of the ECMAScript language. In short, it is also called "ES6".

Although JavaScript is extremely powerful and flexible, it's often criticized for having unnecessary redundancy. Therefore, JavaScript developers often use abstractions such as CoffeeScript and Typescript, which provide easier syntax, powerful features, and compile to JavaScript. ES6 was introduced to improve JavaScript and ensure that developers no longer needed to use abstractions or other techniques to write quality code, which was becoming a lengthy process.

The ES6 features are inherited from other popular and abstracting languages, such as CoffeeScript. Therefore, ES6 language features behave the same way as they do in other languages, and are not new in the programming world, even if they are new in JavaScript.

This book provides explanations with examples for all the features of the new version of ECMAScript, ECMAScript 6. This book is about the JavaScript implementation of ECMAScript 6. All the features and examples in this book work on all the JavaScript environments, such as browsers, Node.js, Cordova, and so on.

What this book covers

Chapter 1, Playing with Syntax, introduces new ways of creating variables and function parameters. This chapter discusses the new objects and functions syntaxes in more depth.

Chapter 2, Knowing Your Library, introduces the new prototype-based methods for the existing objects.

Chapter 3, Using Iterators, shows the different types of iterators available in ES6, and how to create custom iterators. It also discusses the tail call optimization in ES6.

Chapter 4, Asynchronous Programming, illustrates how Promises can make it easier to write code that's executed asynchronously.

Chapter 5, Implementing the Reflect API, gives an in-depth guide to object reflection in ES6.

Chapter 6, Using Proxies, shows how to define the custom behavior the fundamental operations on the objects using the ES6 proxies.

Chapter 7, Walking You Through Classes, introduces the Object-oriented Programming using the ES6 classes. Concepts such as inheritance, constructors, abstraction, information hiding, and more are explained here.

Chapter 8, Modular Programming, explains different ways to create modules using JavaScript. Technologies such as the IIFE, CommonJS, AMD, UMD, and ES6 modules are covered.

What you need for this book

If you are reading this book after ES6 is fully supported by all the JavaScript engines, then you don't need to set up any specific testing environment. You can simply test the examples on any engine of your choice.

If you are reading this book before ES6 is completely supported by all the JavaScript engines, then follow up with this book and execute the code snippets for which you can use an ES6 transpiler. If you want to run the code examples in the browser environment, then use this sample webpage template, which has Traceur transpiler attached to it for converting ES6 into ES5 on every page-load:

```
<!doctype html>
<html>
<head>...</head>
<body>
```

```
...
<script src="traceur.js"></script>
<script src="bootstrap.js"></script>
<script type="module">
          //Place ES6 code here
</script>
</body>
</html>
```

Download the `traceur.js` script from https://google.github.io/traceur-compiler/bin/traceur.js, and the `bootstrap.js` script from https://google.github.io/traceur-compiler/src/bootstrap.js. Then, place them in the same directory as the HTML file containing the previous code.

In the exercise files (the code bundle), Traceur transpiler and polyfills are already attached. The exercise files are created for testing the code examples on browsers.

For *Chapter 4, Asynchronous Programming*, you will have to use the browser environment for testing, as we have used jQuery and AJAX in the examples. You will also need a web server for it.

For *Chapter 8, Modular Programming*, if you use the browser environment for testing, then you need a web server. But if you use the Node.js environment, then you don't need a web server.

Compatibility with ECMAScript 6

This book was written before all the JavaScript engines started supporting all the features of ES6.

The specifications of ES6 have already been finalized. It's just not all JavaScript engines have finished the implementation of all the features of ES6. I am pretty much sure that by the end of 2016, all JavaScript engines will support ES6.

Kangax has created an ES6 compatibility table where you can track the support of various ES6 features on various JavaScript engines. You can find the table at http://kangax.github.io/compat-table/es6/.

Running ECMAScript 6 in incompatible engines

If you want to run ES6 in an engine that doesn't support ES6, then you can use the ES6 polyfills or the ES6 transpilers.

A polyfill is a piece of code that provides the technology that you, the developer, expect the JavaScript engine to provide natively. Remember that polyfills are not available for every ES6 feature, and that they cannot be created. A list of all the available polyfills and their download links are available at `https://github.com/Modernizr/Modernizr/wiki/HTML5-Cross-Browser-Polyfills#ecmascript-6-harmony`.

An ES6 transpiler takes the ES6 source code and outputs the ES5 source code, which is compatible with all JavaScript engines. Transpilers support the conversion of more features than polyfills, but may not support all the features of ES6. There are various transpilers available, such as the Google Traceur (`https://github.com/google/traceur-compiler`), Google Caja (`https://developers.google.com/caja/`), Babel (`https://babeljs.io/`), Termi ES6 Transpiler (`https://github.com/termi/es6-transpiler`), and more. You should always transpile the ES6 code to ES5 before attaching it to your web pages, instead of transpiling it on frontend each time your page loads so that web pages don't load slower.

Therefore, by using a transpiler and/or polyfills, you can start writing ES6 code for distribution even before all the engines completely support ES6 and before non-ES6 engines become obsolete.

Who this book is for

This book is for anyone who is familiar with JavaScript. You don't have to be a JavaScript expert to understand this book. This book will help you take your JavaScript knowledge to the next level.

Conventions

In this book, you will find a number of styles of text that distinguish between different kinds of information. Here are some examples of these styles, and an explanation of their meaning.

Code words in text, database table names, folder names, filenames, file extensions, pathnames, dummy URLs, user input, and Twitter handles are shown as follows: "We can include other contexts through the use of the `include` directive."

A block of code is set as follows:

```
var a = 12; //accessible globally

function myFunction()
{
  console.log(a);

  var b = 13; //accessible throughout function

  if(true)
  {
    var c = 14; //accessible throughout function
    console.log(b);
  }

  console.log(c);
}

myFunction();
```

New terms and **important words** are shown in bold.

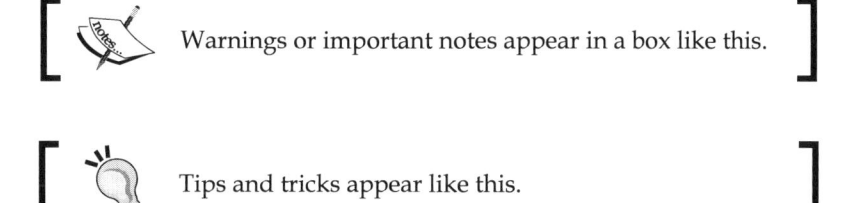

> Warnings or important notes appear in a box like this.

> Tips and tricks appear like this.

Reader feedback

Feedback from our readers is always welcome. Let us know what you think about this book—what you liked or may have disliked. Reader feedback is important for us to develop titles that you really get the most out of.

To send us general feedback, simply send an e-mail to `feedback@packtpub.com`, and mention the book title via the subject of your message.

If there is a topic that you have expertise in and you are interested in either writing or contributing to a book, see our author guide on `www.packtpub.com/authors`.

Customer support

Now that you are the proud owner of a Packt book, we have a number of things to help you to get the most from your purchase.

Downloading the example code

You can download the example code files for all Packt books you have purchased from your account at http://www.packtpub.com. If you purchased this book elsewhere, you can visit http://www.packtpub.com/support and register to have the files e-mailed directly to you.

Errata

Although we have taken every care to ensure the accuracy of our content, mistakes do happen. If you find a mistake in one of our books—maybe a mistake in the text or the code—we would be grateful if you would report this to us. By doing so, you can save other readers from frustration and help us improve subsequent versions of this book. If you find any errata, please report them by visiting http://www.packtpub.com/submit-errata, selecting your book, clicking on the **erratasubmissionform** link, and entering the details of your errata. Once your errata are verified, your submission will be accepted and the errata will be uploaded on our website, or added to any list of existing errata, under the Errata section of that title. Any existing errata can be viewed by selecting your title from http://www.packtpub.com/support.

Piracy

Piracy of copyright material on the Internet is an ongoing problem across all media. At Packt, we take the protection of our copyright and licenses very seriously. If you come across any illegal copies of our works, in any form, on the Internet, please provide us with the location address or website name immediately so that we can pursue a remedy.

Please contact us at copyright@packtpub.com with a link to the suspected pirated material.

We appreciate your help in protecting our authors, and our ability to bring you valuable content.

Questions

You can contact us at questions@packtpub.com if you are having a problem with any aspect of the book, and we will do our best to address it.

1
Playing with Syntax

JavaScript was lacking behind some other programming languages when compared to various syntactic forms such as declaring constant variables, declaring block scoped variables, extracting data from arrays, shorter syntax for declaring functions and so on. **ES6** adds up a lot of new syntax-based features to JavaScript, which helps the developers to write less and do more. ES6 also prevents programmers from using various hacks for achieving various goals, which have negative performance impact and made code harder to read. In this chapter, we will look at the new syntactic features, introduced by ES6.

In this chapter, we'll cover:

- Creating the block scoped variables using the `let` keyword
- Creating constant variables using the `const` keyword
- The spread operator and the rest parameter
- Extracting the data from iterables and objects using the destructuring assignment
- The arrow functions
- The new syntaxes for creating the object properties

The let keyword

The ES6 `let` keyword is used to declare a block scoped variable, optionally initializing it to a value. The programmers who come from other programming language background, but new to JavaScript, often end up writing error-prone JavaScript programs, believing that the JavaScript variables are block scoped. Almost every popular programming language has the same rules when it comes to the variable scopes, but JavaScript acts a bit different due to a lack of the block scoped variables. Due to the fact that JavaScript variables are not block scoped, there are chances of memory leak and also the JavaScript programs are harder to read and debug.

Playing with Syntax

Declaring function scoped variables

The JavaScript variables that are declared using the var keyword are called as **function scoped** variables. The function scoped variables are accessible globally to the script, that is, throughout the script, if declared outside a function. Similarly, if the function scoped variables are declared inside a function, then they become accessible throughout the function, but not outside the function.

Here is an example that shows how to create the function-scoped variables:

```
var a = 12; //accessible globally

function myFunction()
{
  console.log(a);

  var b = 13; //accessible throughout function

  if(true)
  {
    var c = 14; //accessible throughout function
    console.log(b);
  }

  console.log(c);
}

myFunction();
```

The output of the code is:

```
12
13
14
```

> **Downloading the example code**
> You can download the example code files for all Packt books you have purchased from your account at http://www.packtpub.com. If you purchased this book elsewhere, you can visit http://www.packtpub.com/support and register to have the files e-mailed directly to you.

Here, you can see that the c variable is accessible outside the if statement, but this is not the case in other programming languages. So, the programmers coming from other languages would expect the c variable to be undefined outside the if statement, but that's not the case. Therefore, ES6 had introduced the let keyword, which can be used for creating variables that are block scoped.

Declaring block scoped variables

Variables that are declared using the `let` keyword are called as block scoped variables. The block scoped variables behave the same way as the function scoped variables when declared outside a function, that is, they are accessible globally. But when the block scoped variables are declared inside a block, then they are accessible inside the block that they are defined in (and also any sub-blocks) but not outside the block.

 A block is used to group zero or more statements. A pair of curly brackets delimits the block, that is { }.

Let's take the previous example script, replace `var` with the `let` keyword, and see the output:

```
let a = 12; //accessible globally

function myFunction()
{
  console.log(a);

  let b = 13; //accessible throughout function

  if(true)
  {
    let c = 14; //accessible throughout the "if" statement
    console.log(b);
  }

  console.log(c);
}

myFunction();
```

The output of the code is:

```
12
13
Reference Error Exception
```

Now, the output is as expected by a programmer who is used to another programming language.

Re-declaring variables

When you declare a variable using the `var` keyword that is already declared using `var` keyword (in the same scope) then it's overwritten. Consider this example:

```
var a = 0;
var a = 1;

console.log(a);

function myFunction()
{
  var b = 2;
  var b = 3;

  console.log(b);
}

myFunction();
```

The output of the code is:

```
1
3
```

The output is as expected. But the variables created using the `let` keyword don't behave in the same way.

When you declare a variable using the `let` keyword that is already declared using the `let` keyword in the same scope, then it throws a `TypeError` exception. Consider this example:

```
let a = 0;
let a = 1; //TypeError

function myFunction()
{
  let b = 2;
  let b = 3; //TypeError

  if(true)
  {
    let c = 4;
```

```
    let c = 5; //TypeError
  }
}

myFunction();
```

When you declare a variable with a name that's already accessible in a function (or inner function), or is a sub-block using var or the let keyword respectively, then it's a different variable. Here, is an example that shows the behavior:

```
var a = 1;
let b = 2;

function myFunction()
{
  var a = 3; //different variable
  let b = 4; //different variable

  if(true)
  {
    var a = 5; //overwritten
    let b = 6; //different variable

    console.log(a);
    console.log(b);
  }

  console.log(a);
  console.log(b);
}

myFunction();

console.log(a);
console.log(b);
```

The output of the code is:

```
5
6
5
4
1
2
```

Playing with Syntax

> var versus let, which one to use?
> When writing the ES6 code, it is recommended to switch to using the let keyword because it makes scripts more memory friendly, prevents scoping mistakes, prevents accidental bugs, and makes the code easier to read. But if you are already addicted to the var keyword and comfortable using it, then you can still use this.

You may be wondering why not just make the var keyword to define the block-scoped variables instead of introducing the let keyword? The reason why the var keyword wasn't made enough to define block-scoped variables, instead of introducing the let keyword, was for the sake of backward compatibility.

The const keyword

The ES6 const keyword is used to declare the read-only variables, that is, the variables whose value cannot be reassigned. Before ES6, the programmers usually used to prefix the variables that were supposed to be constant. For example, take a look at the following code:

```
var const_pi = 3.141;
var r = 2;
console.log(const_pi * r * r); //Output "12.564"
```

The value of pi should always remain constant. Here, although we have prefixed it, there is still a chance that we might accidentally change its value somewhere in the program, as they're no native protection to the value of pi. Prefixing is just not enough to keep the track of the constant variables.

Therefore, the const keyword was introduced to provide a native protection to the constant variables. So, the previous program should be written in this way in ES6:

```
const pi = 3.141;
var r = 2;

console.log(pi * r * r); //Output "12.564"

pi = 12; //throws read-only exception
```

Here, when we tried to change the value of pi, a read-only exception was thrown.

[6]

The scope of constant variables

Constant variables are block-scoped variables, that is, they follow the same scoping rules as the variables that are declared using the `let` keyword. Here is an example, which shows the scope of the constant variables:

```
const a = 12; //accessible globally

function myFunction()
{
  console.log(a);

  const b = 13; //accessible throughout function

  if(true)
  {
    const c = 14; //accessible throughout the "if" statement
    console.log(b);
  }

  console.log(c);
}

myFunction();
```

The output of the preceding code is:

```
12
13
ReferenceError Exception
```

Here, we can see that the constant variables behave in the same way as the block scoped variables, when it comes to the scoping rules.

Referencing the objects using constant variables

When we assign an object to a variable, the reference of the object is what the variable holds and not the object itself. So, when assigning an object to a constant variable, the reference of the object becomes constant to that variable and not to the object itself. Therefore, the object is mutable.

Playing with Syntax

Consider this example:

```
const a = {
  "name" : "John"
};

console.log(a.name);

a.name = "Eden";

console.log(a.name);

a = {}; //throws read-only exception
```

The output of the preceding code is:

```
John
Eden
a is read only: Exception
```

In this example, the a variable stores the address (that is, reference) of the object. So the address of the object is the value of the a variable, and it cannot be changed. But the object is mutable. So when we tried to assign another object to the a variable, we got an exception as we were trying to change the value of the a variable.

Default parameter values

In JavaScript there is no defined way to assign the default values to the function parameters that are not passed. So, the programmers usually check for the parameters with the undefined value (as it is the default value for the missing parameters), and assign the default values to them. Here is an example, which shows how to do this:

```
function myFunction(x, y, z)
{
  x = x === undefined ? 1 : x;
  y = y === undefined ? 2 : y;
  z = z === undefined ? 3 : z;

  console.log(x, y, z); //Output "6 7 3"
}
myFunction(6, 7);
```

ES6 provides a new syntax that can be used to do this in an easier way. Here is the code which demonstrates how to do this in ES6:

```
function myFunction(x = 1, y = 2, z = 3)
{
  console.log(x, y, z); // Output "6 7 3"
}

myFunction(6,7);
```

Also, passing `undefined` is considered as missing an argument. Here is an example to demonstrate this:

```
function myFunction(x = 1, y = 2, z = 3)
{
  console.log(x, y, z); // Output "1 7 9"
}

myFunction(undefined,7,9);
```

Defaults can also be expressions. Here is an example to demonstrate this:

```
function myFunction(x = 1, y = 2, z = 3 + 5)
{
  console.log(x, y, z); // Output "6 7 8"
}

myFunction(6,7);
```

The spread operator

A spread operator is represented by the "..." token. A spread operator splits an iterable object into the individual values.

> An iterable is an object that contains a group of values, and implements ES6 iterable protocol to let us iterate through its values. An array is an example of built in an iterable object.

Playing with Syntax

A spread operator can be placed wherever multiple function arguments or multiple elements (for array literals) are expected in code.

The spread operator is commonly used to spread the values of an iterable object into the arguments of a function. Let's take an example of an array and see how to split it into the arguments of a function:

Before ES6, for providing the values of an array as function argument, the programmers used the `apply()` method of functions. Here is an example:

```
function myFunction(a, b)
{
   return a + b;
}

var data = [1, 4];
var result = myFunction.apply(null, data);

console.log(result); //Output "5"
```

Here, the apply method takes an array, extracts the values, passes them as individual arguments to the function, and then calls it.

ES6 provides an easy way to do this, using the spread operator. Here is an example:

```
function myFunction(a, b)
{
 return a + b;
}

let data = [1, 4];
let result = myFunction(...data);
console.log(result); //Output "5"
```

During runtime, before the JavaScript interpreter calls the `myFunction` function, it replaces ...data with the 1,4 expression:

```
let result = myFunction(...data);
```

The previous code is replaced with:

```
let result = myFunction(1,4);
```

After this, the function is called.

A spread operator doesn't call the `apply()` method. The JavaScript runtime engine spreads the array using the iteration protocols, and has nothing to do with the `apply()` method, but the behavior is same.

Other usages of the spread operator

The spread operator is not just limited to spreading an iterable object into the function arguments, but it can be used wherever multiple elements (for array literals) are expected in code. So it has many uses. Let's see some other use cases of the spread operator for arrays.

Making array values a part of another array

It can also be used to make the array values a part of another array. Here is an example code that demonstrates how to make the values of an existing array a part of another array while creating it.

```
let array1 = [2,3,4];
let array2 = [1, ...array1, 5, 6, 7];

console.log(array2); //Output "1, 2, 3, 4, 5, 6, 7"
```

Here the following line:

```
let array2 = [1, ...array1, 5, 6, 7];
```

Will be replaced with the following line:

```
let array2 = [1, 2, 3, 4, 5, 6, 7];
```

Pushing the values of an array into another array

Sometimes, we may need to push the values of an existing array into the end of another existing array.

Before ES6, this is how the programmers used to do it:

```
var array1 = [2,3,4];
var array2 = [1];

Array.prototype.push.apply(array2, array1);

console.log(array2); //Output "1, 2, 3, 4"
```

Playing with Syntax

But in ES6 we have a much cleaner way to do it, which is as follows:

```
let array1 = [2,3,4];
let array2 = [1];

array2.push(...array1);

console.log(array2); //Output "1, 2, 3, 4"
```

Here the push method takes a series of variables, and adds them to the end of the array on which it is called.

Here the following line:

```
array2.push(...array1);
```

Will be replaced with the following line:

```
array2.push(2, 3, 4);
```

Spreading multiple arrays

Multiple arrays can be spread on a single line of expression. For example, take the following code:

```
let array1 = [1];
let array2 = [2];
let array3 = [...array1, ...array2, ...[3, 4]];//multi array spread
let array4 = [5];

function myFunction(a, b, c, d, e)
{
   return a+b+c+d+e;
}

let result = myFunction(...array3, ...array4); //multi array spread

console.log(result); //Output "15"
```

The rest parameter

The rest parameter is also represented by the "..." token. The last parameter of a function prefixed with "..." is called as a rest parameter. The rest parameter is an array type, which contains the rest of the parameters of a function when number of arguments exceeds the number of named parameters.

The rest parameter is used to capture a variable number of the function arguments from within a function.

Before ES6, the programmers used the `arguments` object of a function to retrieve the extra arguments, passed to the function. The `arguments` object is not an array, but it provides some interfaces that are similar to an array.

Here is a code example that shows how to use the `arguments` object to retrieve the extra arguments:

```
function myFunction(a, b)
{
  var args = Array.prototype.slice.call(arguments,
  myFunction.length);

  console.log(args);
}

myFunction(1, 2, 3, 4, 5); //Output "3, 4, 5"
```

In ES6, this can be done in a much easier and cleaner way, using the rest parameter. Here is an example of using the rest parameter:

```
function myFunction(a, b, ...args)
{
  console.log(args); //Output "3, 4, 5"
}

myFunction(1, 2, 3, 4, 5);
```

The `arguments` object is not an array object. Therefore, to do array operations on the `arguments` object, you need to first convert it to an array. As the ES6 rest parameter is an array type, it's easier to work with it.

> **What is the "..." token called?**
> The "..." token is called as the spread operator or rest parameter, depending on where and how it's used.

The destructuring assignment

The destructuring assignment is an expression that allows you to assign the values or properties of an iterable or object, to the variables, using a syntax that looks similar to the array or object construction literals respectively.

A destructuring assignment makes it easy to extract data from iterables or objects by providing a shorter syntax. A destructuring assignment is already present in the programming languages, such as **Perl** and **Python**, and works the same way everywhere.

There are two kinds of destructuring assignment expressions—the array and object destructuring assignment. Let's see each of them in details.

The array destructuring assignment

An array destructuring assignment is used to extract the values of an iterable object and assign them to the variables. It's named as the *array destructuring assignment* because the expression is similar to an array construction literal.

Before ES6, the programmers used to do it this way to assign the values of an array to the variables:

```
var myArray = [1, 2, 3];
var a = myArray[0];
var b = myArray[1];
var c = myArray[2];
```

Here, we are extracting the values of an array and assigning them to the a, b, c variables respectively.

In ES6, we can do this in just one line statement using the array destructuring assignment:

```
let myArray = [1, 2, 3];
let a, b, c;

[a, b, c] = myArray; //array destructuring assignment syntax
```

As you see, the `[a, b, c]` is the array destructuring expression.

On the left-hand side of the array destructuring statement, we need to place the variables to which we want to assign the array values, using syntax similar to an array literal. On right-hand side, we need to place an array (actually any iterable object) whose values we want to extract.

The previous example code can be made even shorter in this way:

```
let [a, b, c] = [1, 2, 3];
```

Here we create the variables on the same statement and instead of providing the array variable, we provide the array with a construction literal.

If there are fewer variables than items in the array, then only the first items are considered.

> If you place a non-iterable object on the right-hand side of the array destructuring assignment syntax, then a `TypeError` exception is thrown.

Ignoring values

We can also ignore some of the values of the iterable. Here is example code, which shows how to do this:

```
let [a, , b] = [1, 2, 3];

console.log(a);
console.log(b);
```

The output is as follows:

```
1
3
```

Using the rest operator in the array destructuring assignment

We can prefix the last variable of the array destructuring expression using the "..." token. In this case, the variable is always converted into an array object, which holds the rest of the values of the iterable object, if the number of other variables is less than the values in the iterable object.

Consider this example to understand it:

```
let [a, ...b] = [1, 2, 3, 4, 5, 6];

console.log(a);
console.log(Array.isArray(b));
console.log(b);
```

The output is as follows:

```
1
true
2,3,4,5,6
```

In the previous example code, you can see that the `b` variable is converted into an array, and it holds all the other values of the right-hand side array.

Here the "..." token is called as the **rest operator**.

We can also ignore the values while using the rest operator. Here is an example to demonstrate this:

```
let [a, , ,...b] = [1, 2, 3, 4, 5, 6];

console.log(a);
console.log(b);
```

The output is as follows:

```
1
4,5,6
```

Here, we ignored the `2`, `3` values.

Default values for variables

While destructuring, you can also provide the default values to the variables if an array index is `undefined`. Here is an example to demonstrate this:

```
let [a, b, c = 3] = [1, 2];
console.log(c); //Output "3"
```

Nested array destructuring

We can also extract the values from a multi-dimensional array and assign them to variables. Here is an example to demonstrate this:

```
let [a, b, [c, d]] = [1, 2, [3, 4]];
```

Using the destructuring assignment as a parameter

We can also use the array destructuring expression as the function parameter for extracting the values of an iterable object, passed as argument into the function parameters. Here is an example to demonstrate this:

```
function myFunction([a, b, c = 3])
{
   console.log(a, b, c); //Output "1 2 3"
}

myFunction([1, 2]);
```

Earlier in this chapter, we saw that if we pass `undefined` as an argument to a function call, then JavaScript checks for the default parameter value. So, we can provide a default array here too, which will be used if the argument is `undefined`. Here is an example to demonstrate this:

```
function myFunction([a, b, c = 3] = [1, 2, 3])
{
   console.log(a, b, c);   //Output "1 2 3"
}

myFunction(undefined);
```

Here, we passed `undefined` as an argument and therefore, the default array, which is `[1, 2, 3]`, was used for extracting the values.

The object destructuring assignment

An object destructuring assignment is used to the extract property values of an object and assign them to the variables.

Playing with Syntax

Before ES6, the programmers used to do it in the following way to assign the values of an object's properties to the variables:

```
var object = {"name" : "John", "age" : 23};
var name = object.name;
var age = object.age;
```

In ES6, we can do this in just one line statement, using the object destructuring assignment:

```
let object = {"name" : "John", "age" : 23};
let name, age;

({name, age} = object); //object destructuring assignment syntax
```

On the left-hand side of the object destructuring statement, we need to place the variables to which we want to assign the object property values using syntax similar to object literal. On right-hand side, we need to place an object whose property values we want to extract are finally close the statement using the ( ) token.

Here the variable names must be same as the object property names. If you want to assign different variable names, then you can do it this way:

```
let object = {"name" : "John", "age" : 23};
let x, y;

({name: x, age: y} = object);
```

The previous code can be made even shorter this way:

```
let {name: x, age: y} = {"name" : "John", "age" : 23};
```

Here we are create the variables and object on the same line. We don't need to close the statement using the ( ) token, as we are creating the variables on the same statement.

Default values for the variables

You can also provide the default values to the variables, if the object property is `undefined` while destructuring. Here is an example to demonstrate this:

```
let {a, b, c = 3} = {a: "1", b: "2"};
console.log(c); //Output "3"
```

Destructuring computed property names

Some property names are constructed dynamically using expressions. In this case, to extract the property values, we can use the [ ] token to provide the property name an expression. Here is an example:

```
let {["first"+"Name"]: x} = { firstName: "Eden" };
console.log(x); //Output "Eden"
```

Destructuring nested objects

We can also the extract property values from the nested objects, that is, the objects within the objects. Here is an example to demonstrate this:

```
var {name, otherInfo: {age}} = {name: "Eden", otherInfo: {age: 23}};
console.log(name, age); //Eden 23
```

Using the object destructuring assignment as a parameter

Just like the array destructuring assignment, we can also use the object destructuring assignment as a function parameter. Here is an example to demonstrate this:

```
functionmyFunction({name = 'Eden', age = 23, profession = "Designer"} = {})
{
  console.log(name, age, profession); //Output "John 23 Designer"
}

myFunction({name: "John", age: 23});
```

Here, we passed an empty object as a default parameter value, which will be used as a default object if undefined is passed as a function argument.

The arrow functions

ES6 provides a new way to create functions using the => operator. These functions are called as **arrow** functions. This new method has a shorter syntax, and the arrow functions are the anonymous functions.

Here is an example that shows how to create an arrow function:

```
let circleArea = (pi, r) => {
  let area = pi * r * r;
  return area;
}

let result = circleArea(3.14, 3);

console.log(result); //Output "28.26"
```

Here, `circleArea` is a variable, referencing to the anonymous arrow function. The previous code is similar to the next code in ES5:

```
Var circleArea = function(pi, r) {
  var area = pi * r * r;
  return area;
}

var result = circleArea(3.14, 3);

console.log(result); //Output "28.26"
```

If an arrow function contains just one statement, then you don't have to use the { } brackets to wrap the code. Here is an example:

```
let circleArea = (pi, r) => pi * r * r;
let result = circleArea(3.14, 3);

console.log(result); //Output "28.26"
```

When { } brackets are not used then the value of the statement in the body is automatically returned.

The value of "this" in an arrow function

In the arrow functions, the value of `this` keyword is same as the value of `this` keyword of the enclosing scope (the global or function scope, inside whichever the arrow function is defined), instead of referring to the context object (that is, the object inside of which the function is a property), which is the value of `this` in traditional functions.

Consider this example to understand the difference in the traditional function's and the arrow function's `this` value:

```
var object = {
  f1: function(){
    console.log(this);
    var f2 = function(){ console.log(this); }
    f2();
    setTimeout(f2, 1000);
  }
}

object.f1();
```

The output is as follows:

```
Object
Window
Window
```

Here, `this` inside the `f1` function refers to `object`, as `f1` is the property of it. `this` inside `f2` refers to the `window` object, as `f2` is a property of the `window` object.

But `this` behaves differently in the arrow functions. Let's replace the traditional functions with the arrow functions in the preceding code and see the value of this:

```
var object = {
  f1: () => {
    console.log(this);
    var f2 = () => { console.log(this); }
    f2();
    setTimeout(f2, 1000);
  }
}

object.f1();
```

The output is as follows:

```
Window
Window
Window
```

Here, `this` inside the `f1` function copies the `this` value of global scope, as `f1` lies in global scope. `this` inside `f2` copies the `this` value of `f1`, as `f2` lies in the `f1` scope.

Other differences between the arrow and traditional functions

The arrow functions cannot be used as object constructors that is, the `new` operator cannot be applied on them.

Apart from syntax, the `this` value, and the `new` operator, everything else is the same between the arrow and traditional functions, that is, they both are the instances of the `Function` constructor.

The enhanced object literals

ES6 has added some new syntax-based extensions to the {} object literal for creating properties. Let's see them:

Defining properties

ES6 provides a shorter syntax for assigning the object properties to the values of the variables, which have the same name as the properties.

In ES5, you have been doing this:

```
var x = 1, y = 2;
var object = {
  x: x,
  y: y
};

console.log(object.x); //output "1"
```

In ES6, you can do it this way:

```
let x = 1, y = 2;
let object = { x, y };

console.log(object.x); //output "1"
```

Defining methods

ES6 provides a new syntax for defining the methods on an object. Here is an example to demonstrate the new syntax:

```
let object = {
  myFunction(){
    console.log("Hello World!!!"); //Output "Hello World!!!"
  }
}

object.myFunction();
```

This concise function allows the use of `super` in them, whereas the traditional methods of the objects don't allow the use of `super`. We will learn more about it later in this book.

The computed property names

The property names that are evaluated during runtime are called as the **computed property names**. An expression is usually resolved to find the property name dynamically.

In ES5, the computed properties are defined in this way:

```
var object = {};

object["first"+"Name"] = "Eden";//"firstName" is the property name

//extract
console.log(object["first"+"Name"]); //Output "Eden"
```

Here, after creating the object, we attach the properties to the object. But in ES6, we can add the properties with the computed name while creating the objects. Here is an example:

```
let object = {
  ["first" + "Name"]: "Eden",
};

//extract
console.log(object["first" + "Name"]); //Output "Eden"
```

Summary

In this chapter, we learned about the variable's scopes, read-only variables, splitting arrays into individual values, passing indefinite parameters to a function, extracting data from objects and arrays, arrow functions, and new syntaxes for creating object properties.

In the next chapter, we will learn about built-in objects and symbols, and we will discover the properties added by ES6 into strings, arrays, and objects.

2
Knowing Your Library

ES6 has added lots of new properties and methods to built-in JavaScript objects, so that the programmer can do cumbersome tasks easily. These new functionalities aim to help the developers get rid of using hacks and error-prone techniques to do various operations related to numbers, strings, and arrays. In this chapter, we will look at all the new functionalities added by ES6 to the native objects.

In this chapter, we'll cover:

- The new properties and methods of the `Number` object
- Representing the numeric constants as binary or octal
- The new properties and methods of the `Math` object
- Creating the multiline strings and the new methods of the `String` object
- The new properties and methods of `Array` object
- What are Maps and Sets?
- Using array buffers and typed arrays
- The new properties and methods of `Object` object

Working with numbers

ES6 adds new ways of creating numbers and new properties to the `Number` object to make working with numbers easier. The `Number` object was enhanced in ES6 to make it easier to create mathematically rich applications, and prevent the common misconceptions that caused the errors. ES6 also provides new ways to do things that were already possible in ES5, such as representing the numeric constants as octal.

> JavaScript represents the numbers as base 10 decimals. The numeric constants are, by default, interpreted as base 10 decimals.

The binary notation

In ES5, there was no native way to represent the numeric constants as binary. But in ES6, you can prefix the numeric constants using the `0b` token to make JavaScript interpret them as binary.

Here is an example:

```
let a = 0b00001111;
let b = 15;

console.log(a === b);
console.log(a);
```

The output is as follows:

```
true
15
```

Here, `0b00001111` is a binary representation of 15, base 10 decimal.

The octal notation

In ES5, to represent a numeric constant as octal, we needed to prefix the numeric constant using `0`. For example, take a look at the following:

```
var a = 017;
var b = 15;

console.log(a === b);
console.log(a);
```

The output is as the following:

```
true
15
```

But often, programmers new to JavaScript, get confused with the octal representations as the decimal number with `0` at the front. For example, they think `017` is same as `17`. Therefore, to remove this confusion, ES6 lets us prefix the numeric constants using `0o` to make JavaScript interpret them as octal.

Here is an example to demonstrate this:

```
let a = 0o17;
let b = 15;

console.log(a === b);
console.log(a);
```

The output is as follows:

```
true
15
```

The Number.isInteger(number) method

JavaScript numbers are stored as the 64-bit, floating-point numbers. So the integers in JavaScript are the floating-point numbers without a decimal fraction, or a decimal fraction with all 0's.

In ES5, there was no built-in way to check whether a number is an integer or not. ES6 adds a new method to the `Number` object called as `isInteger()`, which takes a number and returns `true` or `false`, depending on weather the number is an integer or not.

Here is an example code:

```
let a = 17.0;
let b = 1.2;

console.log(Number.isInteger(a));
console.log(Number.isInteger(b));
```

The output is as follows:

```
true
false
```

The Number.isNaN(value) method

In ES5, there was no way to check whether a variable holds the NaN value or not.

> The global isNaN() function is used to check whether a value is a number or not. If the value is not a number, then it returns true, otherwise it returns false.

So ES6 introduced a new method for the Number object called as isNaN() to check whether a value is NaN or not. Here is an example, which demonstrates Number.isNaN() and also explains how it is different from the global isNaN() function:

```
let a = "NaN";
let b = NaN;
let c = "hello";
let d = 12;

console.log(Number.isNaN(a));
console.log(Number.isNaN(b));
console.log(Number.isNaN(c));
console.log(Number.isNaN(d));

console.log(isNaN(a));
console.log(isNaN(b));
console.log(isNaN(c));
console.log(isNaN(d));
```

The output is as follows:

```
false
true
false
false
true
true
true
false
```

Here you can see that Number.isNaN() method returns true only if the passed value is exactly NaN.

> You might ask, why not use == or the === operator instead of the Number.isNaN(value) method? The NaN value is the only value that is not equal to itself, that is, the expression NaN==NaN or NaN===NaN will return false.

The Number.isFinite(number) method

In ES5 there was no built-in way to check whether a value is a finite number.

> The global isFinite() function takes a value and checks whether it's a finite number or not. But unfortunately, it also returns true for values that convert to a Number type.

So ES6 introduced the Number.isFinite() method, which resolves the issue of the window.isFinite() function. Here is an example to demonstrate this:

```
console.log(isFinite(10));
console.log(isFinite(NaN));
console.log(isFinite(null));
console.log(isFinite([]));

console.log(Number.isFinite(10));
console.log(Number.isFinite(NaN));
console.log(Number.isFinite(null));
console.log(Number.isFinite([]));
```

The output is as follows:

```
true
false
true
true
true
false
false
false
```

Knowing Your Library

The Number.isSafeInteger(number) method

The JavaScript numbers are stored as 64-bit floating-point numbers, following the international IEEE 754 standard. This format stores numbers in 64 bits, where the number (the fraction) is stored in 0 to 51 bits, the exponent in 52 to 62 bits, and the sign in the last bit.

So in JavaScript, safe integers are those numbers that are not needed to be rounded to some other integer to fit in the IEEE 754 representation. Mathematically, the numbers from $-(2^{53}-1)$ to $(2^{53}-1)$ are considered as safe integers.

Here is an example to demonstrate this:

```
console.log(Number.isSafeInteger(156));
console.log(Number.isSafeInteger('1212'));
console.log(Number.isSafeInteger(Number.MAX_SAFE_INTEGER));
console.log(Number.isSafeInteger(Number.MAX_SAFE_INTEGER + 1));
console.log(Number.isSafeInteger(Number.MIN_SAFE_INTEGER));
console.log(Number.isSafeInteger(Number.MIN_SAFE_INTEGER - 1));
```

The output is as follows:

```
true
false
true
false
true
false
```

Here, `Number.MAX_SAFE_INTEGER` and `Number.MIN_SAFE_INTEGER` are constant values, introduced in ES6, representing $(2^{53}-1)$ and $-(2^{53}-1)$ respectively.

The Number.EPSILON property

JavaScript uses such binary floating-point representation that the computers fail to accurately represent, numbers like 0.1, 0.2, 0.3, and so on. When your code is executed, numbers like 0.1 are rounded to the nearest number in that format, which results in small rounding error.

Consider this example:

```
console.log(0.1 + 0.2 == 0.3);
console.log(0.9 - 0.8 == 0.1);
console.log(0.1 + 0.2);
console.log(0.9 - 0.8);
```

The output is as follows:

```
false
false
0.30000000000000004
0.09999999999999998
```

The Number.EPSILON property was introduced in ES6, which has a value of approximately 2^{-52}. This value represents a reasonable margin of error when comparing the floating-point numbers. Using this number, we can create a custom function to compare the floating-point numbers by ignoring the minimal rounding errors.

Here is an example code:

```
functionepsilonEqual(a, b)
{
   return Math.abs(a - b) <Number.EPSILON;
}

console.log(epsilonEqual(0.1 + 0.2, 0.3));
console.log(epsilonEqual(0.9 - 0.8, 0.1));
```

The output is as follows:

```
true
true
```

Here, epsilonEqual() is the custom function that we build to compare whether the two values are equal or not. Now, the output is as expected.

> To learn more about this behavior of JavaScript and the floating-point arithmetic, visit http://floating-point-gui.de/.

Doing Math

ES6 adds a lot of new methods to the Math object, related to trigonometry, arithmetic, and miscellaneous. This lets the developers use native methods instead of external math libraries. Native methods are optimized for performance, and have better decimal precision.

Trigonometry related operations

Here is an example code, which shows the entire trigonometry-related methods that are added to the `Math` object:

```
console.log(Math.sinh(0));      //hyberbolic sine of a value
console.log(Math.cosh(0));      //hyberbolic cosine of a value
console.log(Math.tanh(0));      //hyberbolic tangent of a value
console.log(Math.asinh(0));     //inverse hyperbolic sine of a value
console.log(Math.acosh(1));     //inverse hyperbolic cosine of a value
console.log(Math.atanh(0));     //inverse hyperbolic tangent of a value
console.log(Math.hypot(2, 2, 1));//Pythagoras theorem
```

The output is as follows:

```
0
1
0
0
0
0
3
```

Arithmetic related operations

Here is an example code, which shows the entire arithmetic related methods added to the `Math` object:

```
console.log(Math.log2(16));      //log base 2
console.log(Math.log10(1000));   //log base 10
console.log(Math.log1p(0));      //same as log(1 + value)
console.log(Math.expm1(0));      //inverse of Math.log1p()
console.log(Math.cbrt(8));       //cube root of a value
```

The output is as follows:

```
4
3
0
0
2
```

[32]

Miscellaneous methods

ES6 adds some miscellaneous methods to the `Math` object. These methods are used for conversion and extracting information from the numbers.

The Math.imul(number1, number2) function

The `Math.imul()` takes two numbers as 32-bit integers and multiplies them. It returns the lower 32 bits of the result. This is the only native way to do 32-bit integer multiplication in JavaScript.

Here is an example to demonstrate this:

```
console.log(Math.imul(590, 5000000)); //32-bit integer
multiplication
console.log(590 * 5000000); //64-bit floating-point multiplication
```

Output is:

```
-1344967296
2950000000
```

Here when multiplication was done it produced a number so large it couldn't be stored in 32 bits, therefore the lower bits were lost.

The Math.clz32(number) function

The `Math.clz32()` function returns the number of leading zero bits in the 32-bit representation of a number.

Here is an example to demonstrate this:

```
console.log(Math.clz32(7));
console.log(Math.clz32(1000));
console.log(Math.clz32(295000000));
```

Output is:

```
29
22
3
```

The Math.sign(number) function

The `Math.sign()` function returns the sign of a number, indicating weather the number is negative, positive or zero.

Here is an example to demonstrate this:

```
console.log(Math.sign(11));
console.log(Math.sign(-11));
console.log(Math.sign(0));
```

Output is:

```
1
-1
0
```

From the preceding code, we can see that the `Math.sign()` function returns `1` if the number is positive, `-1` if the number is negative, and `0` if the number is zero.

The Math.trunc(number) function

The `Math.trunc()` function returns the integer part of a number by removing any fractional digit. Here is an example to demonstrate this:

```
console.log(Math.trunc(11.17));
console.log(Math.trunc(-1.112));
```

Output is:

```
11
-1
```

The Math.fround(number) function

The `Math.fround()` function rounds a number to a 32-bit floating point value. Here is an example to demonstrate this:

```
console.log(Math.fround(0));
console.log(Math.fround(1));
console.log(Math.fround(1.137));
console.log(Math.fround(1.5));
```

Output is:

```
0
1
1.1369999647140503
1.5
```

Working with strings

ES6 provides new ways of creating strings and adds new properties to global String object and to its instances to make working with strings easier. Strings in JavaScript lacked features and capabilities when compared with programming languages such as Python and **Ruby** therefore ES6 enhanced strings to change that.

Before we get into new string features lets revise JavaScript's internal character encoding and escape sequences. In the Unicode character set every character is represented by a base 10 decimal number called a **code point**. A **code unit** is a fixed number of bits in memory to store a code point. An encoding schema determines the length of code unit. A code unit is 8 bits if the **UTF-8** encoding schema is used or 16 bits if the **UTF-16** encoding schema is used. If a code point doesn't fit in a code unit it is spilt into multiple code units, that is, multiple characters in sequence representing a single character.

JavaScript interpreters by default interpret JavaScript source code as sequence of UTF-16 code units. If source code is written in the UTF-8 encoding schema then there are various ways to tell the JavaScript interpreter to interpret it as sequence of UTF-8 code units. JavaScript strings are always a sequence of UTF-16 code points.

Any Unicode character with a code point less than 65536 can be escaped in a JavaScript string or source code using the hexadecimal value of its code point, prefixed with \u. Escapes are six characters long. They require exactly four characters following \u. If the hexadecimal character code is only one, two or three characters long, you'll need to pad it with leading zeroes. Here is an example to demonstrate this:

```
var \u0061 = "\u0061\u0062\u0063";
console.log(a); //Output is "abc"
```

Escaping larger code points

In ES5, for escaping a character that requires more than 16 bits for storing, we needed two Unicode escapes. For example, to add \u1F691 to a string we had to escape it this way:

```
console.log("\uD83D\uDE91");
```

Here \uD83D and \uDE91 are called **surrogate pairs**. A surrogate pair is two Unicode characters when written in sequence represent another character.

In ES6 we can write it without surrogate pairs:

```
console.log("\u{1F691}");
```

A string stores \u1F691 as \uD83D\uDE91, so length of the above string is still 2

The codePointAt(index) method

The codePointAt() method of a string returns a non-negative integer that is the code point of the character at the given index.

Here is an example to demonstrate this:

```
console.log("\uD83D\uDE91".codePointAt(1));
console.log("\u{1F691}".codePointAt(1));
console.log("hello".codePointAt(2));
```

Output is:

```
56977
56977
1080
```

The String.fromCodePoint(number1, …, number 2) method

The fromCodePoint() method of String object takes a sequence of code points and returns a string. Here is an example to demonstrate this:

```
console.log(String.fromCodePoint(0x61, 0x62, 0x63));
console.log("\u0061\u0062 " == String.fromCodePoint(0x61, 0x62));
```

Output is:

```
abc
true
```

The repeat(count) method

The `repeat()` method of a string, constructs and returns a new string which contains the specified number of copies on which it was called, concatenated together. Here is an example to demonstrate this:

```
console.log("a".repeat(6));      //Output "aaaaaa"
```

The includes(string, index) method

The `includes()` method is used to find whether one string may be found in another string, returning `true` or `false` as appropriate. Here is an example to demonstrate this:

```
var str = "Hi, I am a JS Developer";
console.log(str.includes("JS")); //Output "true"
```

It takes an optional second parameter representing the position in the string at which to begin searching. Here is an example to demonstrate this:

```
var str = "Hi, I am a JS Developer";
console.log(str.includes("JS", 13)); // Output "false"
```

The startsWith(string, index) method

The `startsWith()` method is used to find whether a string begins with the characters of another string, returning `true` or `false` as appropriate. Here is an example to demonstrate this:

```
var str = "Hi, I am a JS Developer";
console.log(str.startsWith('Hi, I am')); //Output "true"
```

It takes an optional second parameter representing the position in the string at which to begin searching. Here is an example to demonstrate this:

```
var str = "Hi, I am a JS Developer";
console.log(str.startsWith('JS Developer', 11)); //Output "true"
```

The endsWith(string, index) function

The `endsWith()` method is used to find whether a string ends with the characters of another string, returning true or false as appropriate. It also takes an optional second parameter representing the position in the string that is assumed as the end of the string. Here is an example to demonstrate this:

```
var str = "Hi, I am a JS Developer";
console.log(str.endsWith("JS Developer"));   //Output "true"
console.log(str.endsWith("JS", 13));         //Output "true"
```

Normalization

Normalization is simply the process of searching and standardizing code points without changing the meaning of the string.

There are also different forms of normalization: NFC, NFD, NFKC and NFKD.

Let's understand Unicode string normalization by an example use case:

A case study

There are many Unicode characters that can be stored in 16 bits and can also be represented using a surrogate pair. For example, 'é' character can be escaped two ways:

```
console.log("\u00E9");    //output 'é'
console.log("e\u0301");   //output 'é'
```

The problem is when applying the == operator, iterating or finding length you will get an unexpected result. Here is an example to demonstrate this:

```
var a = "\u00E9";
var b = "e\u0301";

console.log(a == b);
console.log(a.length);
console.log(b.length);

for(let i = 0; i<a.length; i++)
{
  console.log(a[i]);
}
```

```
for(let i = 0; i<b.length; i++)
{
  console.log(b[i]);
}
```

Output is:

```
false
1
2
é
é◻
```

Here both the strings display the same way but when we do various string operations on them we get different results.

The length property ignores surrogate pairs and assumes every 16-bit to be single character. The `==` operator matches the binary bits therefore it also ignores surrogate pairs. The `[]` operator also assumes every 16-bit to be an index therefore ignoring surrogate pairs.

In this case to solve the problems we need to convert the surrogate pairs to 16-bit character representation. This process is called as **normalization**. To do this ES6 provides a `normalize()` function. Here is an example to demonstrate this:

```
var a = "\u00E9".normalize();
var b = "e\u0301".normalize();

console.log(a == b);
console.log(a.length);
console.log(b.length);

for(let i = 0; i<a.length; i++)
{
  console.log(a[i]);
}

for(let i = 0; i<b.length; i++)
{
  console.log(b[i]);
}
```

Output is:

```
true
1
1
é
é
```

Here the output is as expected. `normalize()` returns the normalized version of the string. `normalize()` uses NFC form by default.

Normalization is not just done in the case of surrogate pairs; there are many other cases.

> The Normalized version of a string is not made for displaying to the user; it's used for comparing and searching in strings.

To learn more about Unicode string normalization and normalization forms visit `http://www.unicode.org/reports/tr15/`

Template strings

Template strings is just a new literal for creating strings that makes various things easier. They provide features such as embedded expressions, multi-line strings, string interpolation, string formatting, string tagging, and so on. They are always processed and converted to a normal JavaScript string on runtime therefore they can be used wherever we use normal strings.

Template strings are written using back ticks instead of single or double quotes. Here is an example of a simple template string:

```
let str1 = `hello!!!`; //template string
let str2 = "hello!!!";

console.log(str1 === str2); //output "true"
```

Expressions

In ES5, to embed expressions within normal strings you would do something like this:

```
Var a = 20;
Var b = 10;
```

```
Var c = "JavaScript";
Var str = "My age is " + (a + b) + " and I love " + c;

console.log(str);
```

Output is:

```
My age is 30 and I love JavaScript
```

In ES6, template strings make it much easier to embed expressions in strings. Template strings can contain expressions in them. The expressions are placed in placeholders indicated by dollar sign and curly brackets, that is, ${expressions}. The resolved value of expressions in the placeholders and the text between them are passed to a function for resolving the template string to a normal string. The default function just concatenates the parts into a single string. If we use a custom function to process the string parts then the template string is called as a **tagged template string** and the custom function is called as **tag function**.

Here is an example which shows how to embed expressions in a template strings:

```
let a = 20;
let b = 10;
let c = "JavaScript";
letstr = `My age is ${a+b} and I love ${c}`;

console.log(str);
```

Output is:

```
My age is 30 and I love JavaScript
```

Let's create a tagged template string, that is, process the string using a tag function. Let's implement the tag function to do the same thing as the default function. Here is an example to demonstrate this:

```
let tag = function(strings, ...values)
{
  let result = "";

  for(let i = 0; i<strings.length; i++)
  {
    result += strings[i];

    if(i<values.length)
    {
      result += values[i];
```

```
      }
   }

   return result;
};

return result;
};

let a = 20;
let b = 10;
let c = "JavaScript";
let str = tag `My age is ${a+b} and I love ${c}`;

console.log(str);
```

Output is:

```
My age is 30 and I love JavaScript
```

Here our tag function's name is `tag` but you can name it anything else. The custom function takes two parameters, that is, the first parameter is an array of string literals of the template string and the second parameter is an array of resolved values of the expressions. The second parameter is passed as multiple arguments therefore we use the rest argument.

Multiline strings

Template strings provide a new way to create strings that contain multiple lines of text.

In ES5, we need to use \n new line character to add new line breaks. Here is an example to demonstrate this:

```
console.log("1\n2\n3");
```

Output is

```
1
2
3
```

In ES6, using **multiline** string we can simply write:

```
console.log(`1
2
3`);
```

Output is:

```
1
2
3
```

In the above code we simply included new lines where we needed to place \n. While converting the template string to normal string the new lines are converted to \n.

Raw strings

A raw string is a normal string in which escaped characters aren't interpreted.

We can create a raw string using a template string. We can get raw version of a template string use String.raw tag function. Here is an example to demonstrate this:

```
let s = String.raw `xy\n${ 1 + 1 }z`;
console.log(s);
```

Output is:

```
xy\n2z
```

Here \n is not interpreted as new line character instead of its two characters, that is, \ and n. Length of variable s would be 6.

If you create a tagged function and you want to return the raw string then use raw property of the first argument. raw property is an array, which holds raw versions of the strings of the first argument. Here is an example to demonstrate this:

```
let tag = function(strings, ...values)
{
    return strings.raw[0]
};

letstr = tag `Hello \n World!!!`;

console.log(str);
```

Output is:

```
Hello \n World!!!
```

Arrays

ES6 adds new properties to the global Array object and to its instances to make working with arrays easier. Arrays in JavaScript lacked features and capabilities when compared with programming languages such as Python and Ruby therefore ES6 enhanced arrays to change that.

The Array.from(iterable, mapFunc, this) method

The `Array.from()` method creates a new array instance from an iterable object. The first argument is a reference to the iterable object. The second argument is optional and is a callback (known as **Map function**) that is called for every element of the iterable object. The third argument is also optional and is the value of `this` inside the Map function.

Here is an example to demonstrate this:

```
letstr = "0123";
letobj = {number: 1};
letarr = Array.from(str, function(value){
    return parseInt(value) + this.number;
}, obj);

console.log(arr);
```

Output is:

```
1, 2, 3, 4
```

The Array.of(values…) method

The `Array.of()` method is an alternative to the `Array` constructor for creating arrays. When using `Array` constructor if we pass only one argument, that too a number, then `Array` constructor constructs an empty array with array `length` property equal to the passed number instead of creating an array of one element with that number in it. Therefore the `Array.of()` method was introduced to resolve this issue.

Here is an example to demonstrate this:

```
let arr1 = new Array(2);
let arr2 = new Array.of(2);

console.log(arr1[0], arr1.length);
console.log(arr2[0], arr2.length);
```

Output is:

```
undefined 2
2 1
```

You should use `Array.of()` instead of `Array` constructor when you are constructing a new array instance dynamically, that is, when you don't know the type of values and the number of elements.

The fill(value, startIndex, endIndex) method

The `fill()` method of an array fills all the elements of the array from the `startIndex` to an `endIndex` (not including `endIndex`) with a given value. Remember that `startIndex` and `endIndex` arguments are optional; therefore if they are not provided then the whole array is filled with the given value. If only `startIndex` is provided then `endIndex` defaults to length of array minus 1.

If `startIndex` is negative then it's treated as length of array plus `startIndex`. If `endIndex` is negative, it is treated as length of array plus `endIndex`.

Here is an example to demonstrate this:

```
let arr1 = [1, 2, 3, 4];
let arr2 = [1, 2, 3, 4];
let arr3 = [1, 2, 3, 4];
let arr4 = [1, 2, 3, 4];
let arr5 = [1, 2, 3, 4];

arr1.fill(5);
arr2.fill(5, 1, 2);
arr3.fill(5, 1, 3);
arr4.fill(5, -3, 2);
arr5.fill(5, 0, -2);
```

Knowing Your Library

```
console.log(arr1);
console.log(arr2);
console.log(arr3);
console.log(arr4);
console.log(arr5);
```

Output is:

```
5,5,5,5
1,5,3,4
1,5,5,4
1,5,3,4
5,5,3,4
```

The find(testingFunc, this) method

The `find()` method of an array returns an array element, if it satisfies the provided testing function. Otherwise it returns `undefined`.

The `find()` method takes two arguments, that is, the first argument is the testing function and the second argument is the value of `this` in the testing function. The second argument is optional.

The testing function has three parameters: the first parameter is the array element being processed, second parameter is the index of the current element being processed and third parameter is the array on which `find()` is called upon.

The testing function needs to return `true` to satisfy a value. The `find()` method returns the first element which satisfies the provided testing function.

Here is an example to demonstrate the `find()` method:

```
var x = 12;
var arr = [11, 12, 13];
var result = arr.find(function(value, index, array){
    if(value == this)
    {
        return true;
    }
}, x);

console.log(result); //Output "12"
```

The findIndex(testingFunc, this) method

The `findIndex()` method is similar to the `find()` method. The `findIndex()` method returns the index of the satisfied array element instead of the element itself.

```
let x = 12;
let arr = [11, 12, 13];
let result = arr.findIndex(function(value, index, array){
    if(value == this)
    {
        return true;
    }
}, x);

console.log(result); Output "1"
```

The copyWithin(targetIndex, startIndex, endIndex) function

The `copyWithin()` method of an array is used to copy the sequence of values of the array to a different position in the array.

The `copyWithin()` method takes three arguments: first argument represents the target index where to copy elements to, second argument represents the index position where to start copying from and the third argument represents the index, that is, where to actually end copying elements.

The third argument is optional and if not provided then it defaults to `length-1` where `length` is the length of the array. If `startIndex` is negative then it's calculated as `length+startIndex`. Similarly if `endIndex` is negative then it's calculated as `length+endIndex`.

Here is an example to demonstrate this:

```
let arr1 = [1, 2, 3, 4, 5];
let arr2 = [1, 2, 3, 4, 5];
let arr3 = [1, 2, 3, 4, 5];
let arr4 = [1, 2, 3, 4, 5];

arr1.copyWithin(1, 2, 4);
arr2.copyWithin(0, 1);
```

Knowing Your Library

```
    arr3.copyWithin(1, -2);
    arr4.copyWithin(1, -2, -1);

    console.log(arr1);
    console.log(arr2);
    console.log(arr3);
    console.log(arr4);
```

Output is:

```
1,3,4,4,5
2,3,4,5,5
1,4,5,4,5
1,4,3,4,5
```

The entries(), keys(), and values() method

The `entries()` method of an array returns an iterable object that contains key/value pairs for each index of the array. Similarly the `keys()` method of an array returns an iterable object that contains keys for each of the indexes in the array. Similarly, the `values()` method of an array returns an iterable object that contains values of the array.

The iterable object returned by the `entries()` method stores the key/value pairs in the form of arrays.

The iterable object returned by these functions is not an array.

Here is an example to demonstrate this:

```
    let arr = ['a', 'b', 'c'];
    let entries = arr.entries();
    let keys = arr.keys();
    let values = arr.values();

    console.log(...entries);
    console.log(...keys);
    console.log(...values);
```

Output is:

```
0,a 1,b 2,c
0 1 2
a b c
```

Collections

A collection is any object that stores multiple elements as a single unit. ES6 introduced various new collection objects to provide better ways of storing and organizing data.

The array is the only collection object available in ES5. ES6 introduces array buffers, typed arrays, Sets, and Maps, which are built in collection objects.

Let's see the different collection objects provided by ES6.

Array buffers

Elements of arrays can be of any type such as strings, numbers, objects, and so on. Arrays can grow dynamically. The problem with arrays is that they are slow in terms of execution time, and occupy more memory. This causes issues while developing applications that require too much computation and deal with large amount of numbers. Therefore array buffers were introduced to tackle this issue.

An array buffer is a collection of 8-bit blocks in memory. Every block is an array buffer element. The size of an array buffer needs to be decided while creating, it therefore it cannot grow dynamically. Array buffers can only store numbers. All blocks are initialized to number 0 on creation of an array buffer.

An array buffer object is created using `ArrayBuffer` constructor.

```
let buffer = new ArrayBuffer(80); //80 bytes size
```

Reading from and writing values into an array buffer object can be done using a DateView object. It's not compulsory that only 8 bits are used to represent a number. We can use 8, 16, 32 and 64 bits to represent a number. Here is an example, which shows how to create a DateView object and read/write to an `ArrayBuffer` object:

```
let buffer = new ArrayBuffer(80);
let view = new DataView(buffer);

view.setInt32(8,22,false);

var number = view.getInt32(8,false);

console.log(number); //Output "22"
```

Knowing Your Library

Here we created a DataView object using `DataView` constructor. A DataView object provides several methods to read and write numbers into an array buffer object. Here we used `setInt32()` method which uses 32 bits to store a provided number.

All the methods of a DataView object that are used to write data to an array buffer object take three arguments. First argument represents the offset, that is, the byte we want to write the number to. Second argument is the number to be stored. And third argument is a Boolean type, which represents the endian of the number, such as `false` represents a big-endian.

Similarly all the methods of a DataView object that are used to read data of an array buffer object take two arguments. First argument is the offset and second argument represents the endian used.

Here are other functions for storing numbers provided by a DataView object:

- **setInt8**: Uses 8 bits to store a number. It takes a signed integer (-ve or +ve).
- **setUint8**: Uses 8 bits to store a number. It takes an unsigned integer (+ve).
- **setInt16**: Uses 16 bits to store a number. It takes a signed integer.
- **setUint16**: Uses 16 bits to store a number. It takes an unsigned integer.
- **setInt32**: Uses 32 bits to store a number. It takes a signed integer.
- **setUint32**: Uses 32 bits to store a number. It takes an unsigned integer.
- **setFloat32**: Uses 32 bits to store a number. It takes a signed decimal number.
- **setFloat64**: Uses 64 bits to store a number. It takes a signed decimal number.

Here are other functions for retrieving stored numbers by a DataView object:

- **getInt8**: Reads 8 bits. Returns signed integer number.
- **getUint8**: Reads 8 bits. Returns unsigned integer number.
- **getInt16**: Reads 16 bits. Returns signed integer number.
- **getUint16**: Reads 16 bits. Returns unsigned integer number.
- **getInt32**: Reads 32 bits. Returns signed integer number.
- **getUint32**: Reads 32 bits. Returns unsigned integer number.
- **getFloat32**: Reads 32 bits. Returns signed decimal number.
- **getFloat64**: Reads 64 bits. Returns signed decimal number.

Typed arrays

We saw how to read and write numbers in array buffers. But the method was very cumbersome because we had to call a function every time. **Typed arrays** let us read and write to an array buffer object just like we do for normal arrays.

A typed array acts like a wrapper for an array buffer object and treats data of an array buffer object as a sequence of *n*-bit numbers. The n value depends on how we created the typed array.

Here is the code example that demonstrates how to create an array buffer object and read/write to it using a typed array:

```
var buffer = new ArrayBuffer(80);
vartyped_array = new Float64Array(buffer);
typed_array[4] = 11;

console.log(typed_array.length);
console.log(typed_array[4]);
```

Output is:

```
10
11
```

Here we created typed array using the `Float64Array` constructor, it therefore treats data in the array buffer as a sequence of 64-bit signed decimal numbers. Here the array buffer object size was 640 bits therefore only 10 64-bit numbers can be stored.

Similarly, there are other typed array constructors to represent data in an array buffer as a sequence of different bit numbers. Here is the list:

- **Int8Array**: Treats as 8-bit signed integers
- **Uint8Array**: Treats as 8-bit unsigned integers
- **Int16Array**: Treats as 16-bit signed integers
- **Uint16Array**: Treats as 16-bit unsigned integers
- **Int32Array**: Treats as 32-bit signed integers
- **Uint32Array**: Treats as 32-bit unsigned integers
- **Float32Array**: Treats as 32-bit signed decimal number
- **Float64Array**: Treats as 64-bit signed decimal number

Typed arrays provide all the methods that are also provided by normal JavaScript arrays. They also implement the iterable protocol therefore they can be used as an iterable object.

Set

A **Set** is a collection of *unique* values of any data type. The values in a Set are arranged in insertion order. A Set is created using `Set` constructor. Here is an example:

```
let set1 = new Set();
let set2 = new Set("Hello!!!");
```

Here `set1` is an empty Set. Whereas `set2` was created using values of an iterable object, that is, characters of a string and the string was not empty therefore `set2` is non-empty.

Here is example code, which demonstrates various operations that can be done on a Set:

```
let set = new Set("Hello!!!");

set.add(12); //add 12

console.log(set.has("!")); //check if value exists
console.log(set.size);

set.delete(12); //delete 12

console.log(...set);

set.clear(); //delete all values
```

Output is:

```
true
6
H e l o !
```

Here we added nine items to the `set` object but the `size` was only six because Set automatically deletes duplicate values. The characters `l` and `!` were repeated multiple times.

The Set object also implements the iterable protocol so they can be used as an iterable object.

Sets are used when you want to maintain a collection of values and check if a value exists instead of retrieving a value. For example: Sets can be used as an alternative to an array if you only use the `indexOf()` method of the array in your code to check if an value exists.

WeakSet

Here are the differences between Set and WeakSet objects:

- A Set can store primitive types and object references whereas a WeakSet object can only store object references
- One of the important features of the WeakSet object is that if there is no other reference to an object stored in a WeakSet object then they are garbage collected
- Lastly a WeakSet object is not enumerable, that is, you cannot find its size; it also doesn't implement iterable protocol

Apart from these three differences it behaves exactly the same way as a Set. Everything else apart from these three differences is same between a Set and WeakSet object.

A WeakSet object is created using `WeakSet` constructor. You cannot pass an iterable object as an argument to WeakSet object.

Here is an example to demonstrate WeakSet:

```
letweakset = new WeakSet();

(function(){
  let a = {};
  weakset.add(a);
})()

//here 'a' is garbage collected from weakset
console.log(weakset.size); //output "undefined"
console.log(...weakset); //Exception is thrown

weakset.clear(); //Exception, no such function
```

Map

A Map is a collection of key/value pairs. Keys and values of a Map can be of any data type. The key/value pairs are arranged in the insertion order. A Map object is created using the `Map` constructor.

Here is an example, which demonstrates how to create a Map object and do various operations on it:

```
let map = new Map();
let o = {n: 1};

map.set(o, "A"); //add
map.set("2", 9);

console.log(map.has("2")); //check if key exists
console.log(map.get(o)); //retrieve value associated with key
console.log(...map);

map.delete("2"); //delete key and associated value
map.clear(); //delete everything

//create a map from iterable object
let map_1 = new Map([[1, 2], [4, 5]]);

console.log(map_1.size); //number of keys
```

Output is:

```
true
A
[object Object],A 2,9
2
```

While creating a Map object from an iterable object we need to make sure that the values returned by the iterable object are arrays, each of length 2 i.e., index 0 is the key and index 1 is the value.

If we try to add a key that already exists then it's overwritten. The Map objects also implement the iterable protocol and can therefore also be used as an iterable object. While iterating Maps using the iterable protocol, they return arrays with key/value pairs as you can see in the preceding example.

WeakMap

Here are the differences between the Map and the WeakMap objects:

- Keys of a Map object can be of primitive types or object references but keys in WeakMap object can only be object references
- One of the important features of the WeakMap object is that if there is no other reference to an object that is referenced by a key then the key is garbage collected.
- Lastly the WeakMap object is not enumerable, that is, you cannot find its size and it doesn't implement iterable protocol.

Everything else, apart from these three differences is similar between the Map and the WeakMap object.

A WeakMap is created using `WeakMap` constructor. Here is an example that demonstrates its usage:

```
let weakmap = new WeakMap();

(function(){
  let o = {n: 1};
  weakmap.set(o, "A");
})()

//here 'o' key is garbage collected
let s = {m: 1};

weakmap.set(s, "B");

console.log(weakmap.get(s));
console.log(...weakmap); //exception thrown

weakmap.delete(s);
weakmap.clear(); //Exception, no such function

let weakmap_1 = new WeakMap([[{}, 2], [{}, 5]]);   //this works

console.log(weakmap_1.size); //undefined
```

Object

ES6 standardizes the __proto__ property of an object and adds new properties to the global `Object` object.

The __proto__ property

JavaScript objects have an internal `[[prototype]]` property that references the object's prototype, that is, the object it inherits. To read the property we had to use `Object.getPrototypeof()` and to create a new object with a given prototype we had to use the `Object.create()` method. A `[[prototype]]` property cannot be directly read or be modified.

Inheriting was cumbersome due to the nature of the `[[prototype]]` property, therefore some browsers added a special __proto__ property in objects, which is an accessor property that exposes the internal `[[prototype]]` property and makes working with prototypes easier. The __proto__ property was not standardized in ES5 but due to its popularity it was standardized in ES6.

Here is an example to demonstrate this:

```
//In ES5
var x = {x: 12};
var y = Object.create(x, {y: {value: 13}});

console.log(y.x); //Output "12"
console.log(y.y); //Output "13"

//In ES6
let a = {a: 12, __proto__: {b: 13}};
console.log(a.a); //Output "12"
console.log(a.b); //Output "13"
```

The Object.is(value1, value2) method

The `Object.is()` method determines whether two values are equal or not. It is similar to the `===` operator but there are some special cases for the `Object.is()` method. Here is an example that demonstrates the special cases:

```
console.log(Object.is(0, -0));
console.log(0 === -0);
console.log(Object.is(NaN, 0/0));
```

```
console.log(NaN === 0/0);
console.log(Object.is(NaN, NaN));
console.log(NaN ===NaN);
```

Output is:

```
false
true
true
false
true
false
```

The Object.setPrototypeOf(object, prototype) method

The `Object.setPrototypeOf()` method is just an another way to assign the `[[prototype]]` property of an object. Here is an example to demonstrate this:

```
let x = {x: 12};
let y = {y: 13};

Object.setPrototypeOf(y, x)

console.log(y.x); //Output "12"
console.log(y.y); //Output "13"
```

The Object.assign(targetObj, sourceObjs...) method

The `Object.assign()` method is used is used to copy the values of all enumerable own properties from one or more source objects to a target object. This method will return the `targetObj`.

Here is an example which demonstrates this:

```
let x = {x: 12};
let y = {y: 13, __proto__: x};
let z = {z: 14, get b() {return 2;}, q: {}};

Object.defineProperty(z, "z", {enumerable: false});

let m = {};
```

```
Object.assign(m, y, z);

console.log(m.y);
console.log(m.z);
console.log(m.b);
console.log(m.x);
console.log(m.q == z.q);
```

Output is:

```
13
undefined
2
undefined
true
```

Here is a list of important things to keep in mind while using the `Object.assign()` method:

- It invokes getters on the sources and setters on the target.
- It just assigns values of the properties of source to the new or existing properties of target.
- It doesn't copy the `[[prototype]]` property of sources.
- JavaScript property names can be strings or symbols. `Object.assign()` copies both.
- Property definitions are not copied from sources therefore you need to use `Object.getOwnPropertyDescriptor()` `Object.defineProperty()` instead.
- It ignores copying keys with `null` and `undefined` values.

Summary

In this chapter we learned new features added by ES6 for working with numbers, strings, arrays and objects. We saw how arrays impact performance in math-rich applications and how the array buffers can be used instead. We also walked through the new collection objects provided by ES6.

In next chapter, we will learn about Symbols and Iteration protocol, and we will discover `yield` keyword and generators also.

3
Using Iterators

ES6 introduces new object interfaces and loops for iteration. The addition of the new iteration protocols opens up a new world of algorithms and abilities for JavaScript. We will start the chapter by introducing the symbols and various properties of the `Symbol` object. We will also learn how the execution stacks are created for the nested function calls, their impacts, and how to optimize their performance and memory usage.

Although symbols are a separate topic to iterators, we will still be covering symbols in this chapter because to implement the iterable protocol, you need to use symbols.

In this chapter, we'll cover:

- Using symbols as the object property keys
- Implementing the iteration protocols in the objects
- Creating and using the generator objects
- Using the `for...of` loop for iterating
- The tail call optimization

The ES6 symbols

ES6 symbols are the new primitive type introduced in ES6. A symbol is a unique and immutable value. Here is an example code, which shows how to create a symbol:

```
var s = Symbol();
```

Symbols don't have a literal form; therefore, we need to use the `Symbol()` function to create a symbol. The `Symbol()` function returns a unique symbol every time it is called.

Using Iterators

The `Symbol()` function takes an optional string parameter that represents the description of the symbol. A description of a symbol can be used for debugging, but not to access the symbol itself. Two symbols with the same description are not equal at all. Here is an example to demonstrate this:

```
let s1 = window.Symbol("My Symbol");
let s2 = window.Symbol("My Symbol");

console.log(s1 === s2); //Output is "false"
```

From the preceding example, we can also say that a symbol is a *string-like* value that can't collide with any other value.

The "typeof" operator

The `typeof` operator outputs `"symbol"` when applied on a variable, holding a symbol. Here is an example to demonstrate this:

```
var s = Symbol();
console.log(typeof s); //Output "symbol"
```

Using the `typeof` operator is the only way to identify whether a variable is holding a symbol.

The "new" operator

You cannot apply the `new` operator on the `Symbol()` function. The `Symbol()` function detects if it's being used as an constructor, and if `true`, it then throws an exception. Here is an example to demonstrate this:

```
try
{
   let s = new Symbol(); //"TypeError" exception
}
catch(e)
{
   console.log(e.message); //Output "Symbol is not a constructor"
}
```

But the JavaScript engine can internally use the `Symbol()` function as an constructor to wrap a symbol in an object. Therefore, "s" will be equal to `Object(s)`.

> All the primitive types that are introduced from ES6 onwards will not allow their constructors to be invoked manually.

Using symbols as property keys

Till ES5, the JavaScript object property keys had to be string type. But in ES6, the JavaScript object property keys can be strings or symbols. Here is an example that demonstrates how to use a symbol as an object property key:

```
let obj = null;
let s1 = null;

(function(){
  let s2 = Symbol();
  s1 = s2;
  obj = {[s2]: "mySymbol"}
  console.log(obj[s2]);
  console.log(obj[s2] == obj[s1]);
})();

console.log(obj[s1]);
```

The output is:

```
mySymbol
true
mySymbol
```

From the preceding code, you can see that in order to create or retrieve a property key using symbols, you need to use the `[]` token. We saw the `[]` token while discussing the computed property names in *Chapter 2, Knowing Your Library*.

To access a symbol property key, we need the symbol. In the previous example, both `s1` and `s2` hold the same symbol value.

> The primary reason for introducing symbols in ES6 was so that it can be used as a key for object property, and prevent the accidental collision of the property keys.

Using Iterators

The Object.getOwnPropertySymbols() method

The `Object.getOwnPropertyNames()` method cannot retrieve the symbol properties. Therefore, ES6 introduced `Object.getOwnPropertySymbols()` to retrieve an array of symbol properties of an object. Here is an example to demonstrate this:

```
let obj = {a: 12};
let s1 = Symbol("mySymbol");
let s2 = Symbol("mySymbol");

Object.defineProperty(obj, s1, {
  enumerable: false
});

obj[s2] = "";

console.log(Object.getOwnPropertySymbols(obj));
```

The output is as follows:

```
Symbol(mySymbol),Symbol(mySymbol)
```

From the previous example, you can see that the `Object.getOwnPropertySymbols()` method can also retrieve the non-enumerable symbol properties.

> The `in` operator can find the symbol properties in an object, whereas the `for...in` loop and `Object.getOwnPropertyNames()` cannot find the symbol properties in an object for the sake of backward compatibility.

The Symbol.for(string) method

The `Symbol` object maintains a registry of the key/value pairs, where the key is the symbol description, and the value is the symbol. Whenever we create a symbol using the `Symbol.for()` method, it gets added to the registry and the method returns the symbol. If we try to create a symbol with a description that already exists, then the existing symbol will be retrieved.

The advantage of using the `Symbol.for()` method instead of the `Symbol()` method to create symbols is that while using the `Symbol.for()` method, you don't have to worry about making the symbol available globally, because its always available globally. Here is an example to demonstrate this:

```
let obj = {};

(function(){
  let s1 = Symbol("name");
  obj[s1] = "Eden";
})();

//obj[s1] cannot be accessed here

(function(){
  let s2 = Symbol.for("age");
  obj[s2] = 27;
})();

console.log(obj[Symbol.for("age")]); //Output "27"
```

The well-known symbols

In addition to your own symbols, ES6 comes up with a built-in set of symbols, known as the **well-known** symbols. Here is a list of properties, referencing some important built-in symbols:

- `Symbol.iterator`
- `Symbol.match`
- `Symbol.search`
- `Symbol.replace`
- `Symbol.split`
- `Symbol.hasInstance`
- `Symbol.species`
- `Symbol.unscopables`
- `Symbol.isContcatSpreadable`
- `Symbol.toPrimitive`
- `Symbol.toStringTag`

Using Iterators

You will come across the use of these symbols in various chapters of this book.

> While referring to the well-known symbols in the text, we usually prefix them using the @@ notation. For example, the Symbol.iterator symbol is referred to as the @@iterator method. This is done to make it easier to refer to the well-known symbols in the text.

The iteration protocols

An iteration protocol is a set of rules that an object needs to follow for implementing the interface, which when used, a loop or a construct can iterate over a group of values of the object.

ES6 introduces two new iteration protocols known as the **iterable protocol**, and the iterator protocol.

The iterator protocol

Any object that implements the iterator protocol is known as an iterator. According to the iterator protocol, an object needs to provide a `next()` method that returns the next item in the sequence of a group of items.

Here is an example to demonstrate this:

```
let obj = {
  array: [1, 2, 3, 4, 5],
  nextIndex: 0,
  next: function(){
     return this.nextIndex < this.array.length ?
     {value: this.array[this.nextIndex++], done: false} :
     {done: true};
  }
};

console.log(obj.next().value);
console.log(obj.next().value);
console.log(obj.next().value);
console.log(obj.next().value);
console.log(obj.next().value);
console.log(obj.next().done);
```

The output is as follows:

```
1
2
3
4
5
true
```

Every time the `next()` method is called, it returns an object with two properties: `value` and `done`. Let's see what these two properties represent:

- The `done` property: This returns `true` if the iterator has finished iterating over the collection of values. Otherwise, this returns as `false`.
- The `value` property: This holds the value of the current item in the collection. It is omitted when the `done` property is `true`.

The iterable protocol

Any object that implements the iterable protocol is known as an iterable. According to the iterable protocol, an object needs to provide the `@@iterator` method; that is, it must have the `Symbol.iterator` symbol as a property key. The `@@iterator` method must return an iterator object.

Here is an example to demonstrate this:

```
let obj = {
  array: [1, 2, 3, 4, 5],
  nextIndex: 0,
  [Symbol.iterator]: function(){
    return {
      array: this.array,
      nextIndex: this.nextIndex,
      next: function(){
        return this.nextIndex < this.array.length ?
        {value: this.array[this.nextIndex++], done: false} :
        {done: true};
      }
    }
  }
};

let iterable = obj[Symbol.iterator]()
```

Using Iterators

```
console.log(iterable.next().value);
console.log(iterable.next().value);
console.log(iterable.next().value);
console.log(iterable.next().value);
console.log(iterable.next().value);
console.log(iterable.next().done);
```

The output is as follows:

```
1
2
3
4
5
true
```

Generators

A generator function is like a normal function, but instead of returning a single value, it returns multiple values one by one. Calling a generator function doesn't execute its body immediately, but rather returns a new instance of the generator object (that is, an object that implements both, iterable and iterator protocols).

Every generator object holds a new execution context of the generator function. When we execute the `next()` method of the generator object, it executes the generator function's body until the `yield` keyword is encountered. It returns the yielded value, and pauses the function. When the `next()` method is called again, it resumes the execution, and then returns the next yielded value. The `done` property is true when the generator function doesn't yield any more value.

A generator function is written using the `function*` expression. Here is an example to demonstrate this:

```
function* generator_function()
{
  yield 1;
  yield 2;
  yield 3;
  yield 4;
  yield 5;
}

let generator = generator_function();
```

```
console.log(generator.next().value);
console.log(generator.next().value);
console.log(generator.next().value);
console.log(generator.next().value);
console.log(generator.next().value);
console.log(generator.next().done);

generator = generator_function();

let iterable = generator[Symbol.iterator]();

console.log(iterable.next().value);
console.log(iterable.next().value);
console.log(iterable.next().value);
console.log(iterable.next().value);
console.log(iterable.next().value);
console.log(iterable.next().done);
```

The output is as follows:

```
1
2
3
4
5
true
1
2
3
4
5
true
```

There is an expression following the `yield` keyword. The value of the expression is what returned by the generator function via the iterable protocol. If we omit the expression, then `undefined` is returned. The value of the expression is what we call as the yielded value.

We can also pass an optional argument to the `next()` method. This argument becomes the value returned by the `yield` statement, where the generator function is currently paused. Here is an example to demonstrate this:

```
function* generator_function()
{
  var a = yield 12;
```

Using Iterators

```
  var b = yield a + 1;
  var c = yield b + 2;
  yield c + 3;
}

var generator = generator_function();

console.log(generator.next().value);
console.log(generator.next(5).value);
console.log(generator.next(11).value);
console.log(generator.next(78).value);
console.log(generator.next().done);
```

The output is as follows:

```
12
6
13
81
true
```

The return(value) method

You can anytime end a generator function before it has yielded all the values using the `return()` method of the generator object. The `return()` method takes an optional argument, representing the final value to return.

Here is an example demonstrating this:

```
function* generator_function()
{
  yield 1;
  yield 2;
  yield 3;
}

var generator = generator_function();

console.log(generator.next().value);
console.log(generator.return(22).value);
console.log(generator.next().done);
```

The output is as follows:

```
1
22
true
```

The throw(exception) method

You can manually trigger an exception inside a generator function using the `throw()` method of the generator object. You must pass an exception to the `throw()` method that you want to throw. Here is an example to demonstrate this:

```
function* generator_function()
{

  try
  {
    yield 1;
  }
  catch(e)
  {
    console.log("1st Exception");
  }

  try
  {
    yield 2;
  }
  catch(e)
  {
    console.log("2nd Exception");
  }

}

var generator = generator_function();

console.log(generator.next().value);
console.log(generator.throw("exception string").value);
console.log(generator.throw("exception string").done);
```

Using Iterators

The output is as follows:

```
1
1st Exception
2
2nd Exception
true
```

In the preceding example, you can see that the exception is thrown where the function was paused the last time. After the exception is handled, the `throw()` method continuous execution, and returns the next yielded value.

The "yield*" keyword

The `yield*` keyword inside a generator function takes an iterable object as the expression and iterates it to yield its values. Here is an example to demonstrate this:

```
function* generator_function_1()
{
  yield 2;
  yield 3;
}

function* generator_function_2()
{
  yield 1;
  yield* generator_function_1();
  yield* [4, 5];
}

var generator = generator_function_2();

console.log(generator.next().value);
console.log(generator.next().value);
console.log(generator.next().value);
console.log(generator.next().value);
console.log(generator.next().value);
console.log(generator.next().done);
```

The output is as follows:

```
1
2
3
```

```
4
5
true
```

The "for...of" loop

Until now, we were iterating over an iterable object using the `next()` method, which is a cumbersome task. ES6 introduced the for...of loop to make this task easier.

The for...of loop was introduced to iterate over the values of an iterable object. Here is an example to demonstrate this:

```
function* generator_function()
{
  yield 1;
  yield 2;
  yield 3;
  yield 4;
  yield 5;
}

let arr = [1, 2, 3];

for(let value of generator_function())
{
  console.log(value);
}

for(let value of arr)
{
  console.log(value);
}
```

The output is as follows:

```
1
2
3
4
5
1
2
3
```

The tail call optimization

Whenever a function call is made, an execution stack is created in the stack memory to store the variables of the function.

When a function call is made inside another function call, a new execution stack is created for the inner function call. But the problem is that the inner function execution stack takes up some extra memory, that is, it stores an extra address, representing where to resume the execution when this function finishes executing. Switching and creating the execution stacks also takes some additional CPU time. This problem is not noticeable when there are a couple or hundreds of nested levels of calls, but it's noticeable when there are thousands or more of the nested levels of calls, that is, the JavaScript engines throw the `RangeError: Maximum call stack size exceeded` exception. You might have, at some point, experienced the `RangeError` exception while creating a recursive function.

A **tail call** is a function call, performed optionally at the very end of a function with the `return` statement. If a tail call leads to the same function call again and again, then it's called as a **tail-recursion**, which is a special case of recursion. What's special about tail calls is that there is a way to actually prevent the extra CPU-time and memory usage while making the tail calls, which is to reuse the stack of the out function, instead of creating a new execution stack thereby saving the CPU time and the extra memory usage. Reusing the execution stack while making a tail call is called as the **tail call optimization**.

ES6 adds the support for a tail call optimization if the script is written in the `"use strict"` mode. Let's see an example of a tail call:

```
"use strict";

function _add(x, y)
{
  return x + y;
}

function add1(x, y)
{
  x = parseInt(x);
  y = parseInt(y);

  //tail call
  return _add(x, y);
}
```

```
function add2(x, y)
{
  x = parseInt(x);
  y = parseInt(y);

  //not tail call
  return 0 + _add(x, y);
}

console.log(add1(1, '1')); //2
console.log(add2(1, '2')); //3
```

Here, the _add() call in the add1() function is a tail call, as it's the final action of the add1() function. But the _add() call in the add2() function is not a tail call, as it's not the final action, which is adding 0 to the result of _add() is the final action.

The _add() call in add1() doesn't create a new execution stack. Instead, it reuses the add1() function's execution stack; in other words, the tail call optimization occurs.

Converting the non-tail calls into the tail calls

As the tail calls are optimized, you must use the tail calls whenever possible, instead of the non-tail calls. You can optimize your code by converting the non-tail calls into the tail calls.

Let's see an example of converting a non-tail call into a tail call, which is similar to the previous

```
"use strict";

function _add(x, y)
{
  return x + y;
}

function add(x, y)
{
  x = parseInt(x);
  y = parseInt(y);

  var result = _add(x, y);
  return result;
}

console.log(add(1, '1'));
```

In the previous code, the _add() call was not a tail call and therefore, two execution stacks were created. We can convert it into a tail call in this way:

```
function add(x, y)
{
  x = parseInt(x);
  y = parseInt(y);

  return _add(x, y);
}
```

Here, we omitted the use of the `result` variable and instead, we lined up the function call with the `return` statement. Similarly, there are many other strategies to convert the non-tail calls into the tail calls.

Summary

In this chapter, we learned a new way of creating the object property keys using symbols. We saw the iterator and iterable protocols, and learned how to implement these protocols in the custom objects. Then, we learned how to iterate over an iterable object using the `for...of` loop. Finally, we ended the chapter by learning what tail calls are, and how they are optimized in ES6.

In the next chapter, we will learn what Promises are, and how to write a better asynchronous code using Promises.

4
Asynchronous Programming

ES6 introduced a native support for the well-known programming patterns. One such pattern is the Promise pattern, which makes it easier to read and write the asynchronous code. In this chapter, we will learn to write asynchronous code using the ES6 Promise API. The new JavaScript and **HTML5** asynchronous APIs are now being implemented with Promises to facilitate writing less and cleaner code. Therefore, it's important to learn Promises in-depth. We will also see some example APIs that are exposed using Promises such as the **Web Cryptography API**, and the **Battery Status API**.

In this chapter, we'll cover:

- The JavaScript execution model
- The difficulties faced while writing the asynchronous code
- Creating Promises and how Promises work
- How Promises make it easier to write the asynchronous code
- The different states of a Promise
- Various methods of the Promise object.
- Various JavaScript and HTML5 APIs, which use Promises

The JavaScript execution model

The JavaScript code is executed in a single thread, that is, two pieces of script cannot run at same time. Each website opened in browser gets a single thread for downloading, parsing, and executing the website called as the main thread.

The main thread also maintains a queue, which has asynchronous tasks queued to be executed one by one. These queued tasks can be event handlers, callbacks, or any other kind of task. The new tasks are added to the queue as **AJAX** requests/response happen, events occur, timers registered, and more. One long running queue task can stop the execution of all other queue tasks and the main script. The main thread executes the tasks of this queue whenever possible.

> HTML5 introduced **web workers**, which are the actual threads running parallel to the main thread. When a web worker finishes executing or needs to notify the main thread, it simply adds a new event item to the queue.

This queue is what makes it possible for executing the code asynchronously.

Writing asynchronous code

ES5 natively supports two patterns for writing the asynchronous code, that is, the event pattern and the callback pattern. While writing the asynchronous code, we usually start an asynchronous operation and register the event handlers or pass the callbacks, which will be executed once the operation is finished.

The event handlers or the callbacks are used, depending on how the specific asynchronous API is designed. An API that is designed for an event pattern can be wrapped with some custom code to create the callback pattern for the API, and vice-versa. For example, AJAX is designed for the event pattern, but **jQuery** AJAX exposes it as a callback pattern.

Let's consider some examples of writing asynchronous code involving events and callbacks and their difficulties.

The asynchronous code involving events

For asynchronous JavaScript APIs involving events, you need to register the success and error event handlers which will be executed depending on whether the operation was a success or failure respectively.

For example, while making an AJAX request, we register the event handlers which will be executed depending on whether the AJAX request was made successfully or not. Consider this code snippet which makes and AJAX request and logs the retrieved information:

```
function displayName(json)
{
  try
  {
    //we usally display it using DOM
    console.log(json.Name);
  }
  catch(e)
  {
    console.log("Exception: " + e.message);
  }
}
function displayProfession(json)
{
  try
  {
    console.log(json.Profession);
  }
  catch(e)
  {
    console.log("Exception: " + e.message);
  }
}

function displayAge(json)
{
  try
  {
    console.log(json.Age);
  }
  catch(e)
  {
```

```javascript
      console.log("Exception: " + e.message);
    }
}

function displayData(data)
{
  try
  {
    var json = JSON.parse(data);

    displayName(json);
    displayProfession(json);
    displayAge(json);
  }
  catch(e)
  {
    console.log("Exception: " + e.message);
  }
}

var request = new XMLHttpRequest();
var url = "data.json";

request.open("GET", url);
request.addEventListener("load", function(){
  if(request.status === 200)
  {
    displayData(request.responseText);
  }
  else
  {
    console.log("Server Error: " + request.status);
  }
}, false);

request.addEventListener("error", function(){
  console.log("Cannot Make AJAX Request");
}, false);

request.send();
```

Here, we assume the data.json file to have this content:

```
{
  "Name": "Eden",
  "Profession": "Developer",
  "Age": "25"
}
```

The send() method of the XMLHttpRequest object is executed asynchronously, which retrieves the data.json file and calls the load or error event handler, depending on whether the request was made successfully or not.

There is absolutely no issue with how this AJAX works, but the issue is with how we write the code involving events. Here are the issues that we faced while writing the previous code:

- We had to add an exception handler for every block of code that will be executed asynchronously. We can't just wrap the whole code using a single try...catch statement. This makes it difficult to catch the exceptions.
- The code is harder to read, as it's difficult to follow the code flow due to the nested function calls.
- If another part of the program wants to know if the asynchronous operation is finished, pending, or being executed then we have to maintain the custom variables for that purpose. So we can say it is difficult to find the state of the asynchronous operation.

This code can get even more complicated and harder to read if you are nesting multiple AJAX or any other asynchronous operations. For example, after displaying the data, you may want to ask the user to verify if the data is correct or not and then send the Boolean value back to the server. Here is the code example to demonstrate this:

```
function verify()
{
  try
  {
    var result = confirm("Is the data correct?");
    if (result == true)
    {
      //make AJAX request to send data to server
    }
    else
    {
      //make AJAX request to send data to server
    }
```

[79]

Asynchronous Programming

```
  }
  catch(e)
  {
    console.log("Exception: " + e.message);
  }
}

function displayData(data)
{
  try
  {
    var json = JSON.parse(data);

    displayName(json);
    displayProfession(json);
    displayAge(json);

    verify();
  }
  catch(e)
  {
    console.log("Exception: " + e.message);
  }
}
```

The asynchronous code involving callbacks

For asynchronous JavaScript APIs involving callbacks, you need to pass the success and error callbacks, which will be called depending on whether the operation was a success or failure respectively.

For example, while making an AJAX request using jQuery, we need to pass the callbacks, which will be executed depending on whether the AJAX request was made successfully or not. Consider this code snippet that makes an AJAX request using jQuery and logs the retrieved information:

```
function displayName(json)
{
  try
  {
    console.log(json.Name);
  }
  catch(e)
  {
```

```
      console.log("Exception: " + e.message);
  }
}

function displayProfession(json)
{
  try
  {
    console.log(json.Profession);
  }
  catch(e)
  {
    console.log("Exception: " + e.message);
  }
}

function displayAge(json)
{
  try
  {
    console.log(json.Age);
  }
  catch(e)
  {
    console.log("Exception: " + e.message);
  }
}

function displayData(data)
{
  try
  {
    var json = JSON.parse(data);

    displayName(json);
    displayProfession(json);
    displayAge(json);
  }
  catch(e)
  {
    console.log("Exception: " + e.message);
  }
}
```

```
$.ajax({url: "data.json", success: function(result, status,
responseObject){
    displayData(responseObject.responseText);
}, error: function(xhr,status,error){
    console.log("Cannot Make AJAX Request. Error is: " + error);
}});
```

Even here, there is absolutely no issue with how this jQuery AJAX works, but the issue is with how we write the code involving callbacks. Here are the issues that we faced while writing the preceding code:

- It is difficult to catch the exceptions, as we have to use multiple `try` and `catch` statements.
- The code is harder to read, as it's difficult to follow the code flow due to the nested function calls.
- It's difficult to maintain the state of the asynchronous operation.

Even this code will get more complicated if we nest the multiple jQuery AJAX or any other asynchronous operations.

Promises to the rescue

ES6 introduces a new native pattern for writing the asynchronous code called as Promise pattern.

This new pattern removes the common code issues that the event and callback pattern had. It also makes the code look more like a synchronous code.

A Promise (or a Promise object) represents an asynchronous operation. The existing asynchronous JavaScript APIs are usually wrapped with Promises, and the new JavaScript APIs are being purely implemented using the Promises.

Promises are new in JavaScript but are already present in many other programming languages. Programming Languages such as C# 5, C++ 11, Swift, Scala, and more are some examples that support Promises.

ES6 provides the Promise API using which we can create Promises and use them. Let's explore the ES6 Promise API.

The Promise constructor

The `Promise` constructor is used to create new Promise instances. A Promise object represents an asynchronous operation.

We need to pass a callback to the `Promise` constructor, which executes the asynchronous operation. This callback is called as the **executor**. The executor should take two parameters, that is, the `resolve` and `reject` callbacks. The `resolve` callback should be executed if the asynchronous operation was successful, and the `reject` callback should be executed if the operation was unsuccessful. If the asynchronous operation was successful and has a result, then we can pass the result of the asynchronous operation to the `resolve` callback. If the asynchronous operation was unsuccessful, then we can pass the reason of failure to the `reject` callback.

Here is a code example, which demonstrates how to create a Promise and wrap an AJAX request using it:

```
var promise = new Promise(function(resolve, reject){

   var request = new XMLHttpRequest();
   var url = "data.json";

   request.open("GET", url);

   request.addEventListener("load", function(){
     if(request.status === 200)
     {
       resolve(request.responseText);
     }
     else
     {
       reject("Server Error: " + request.status);
     }
   }, false);

   request.addEventListener("error", function(){
     reject("Cannot Make AJAX Request");
   }, false);

   request.send();

});
```

The executor is executed synchronously. But the executor is executing an asynchronous operation and therefore, the executor can return before the asynchronous operation is finished.

A Promise is always in one of these states:

- **Fulfilled**: If the `resolve` callback is invoked with a non-Promise object as argument or no argument, then we say that the Promise is fulfilled
- **Rejected**: If the `reject` callback is invoked or an exception occurs in the executor scope, then we say that the Promise is rejected
- **Pending**: If the `resolve` or `reject` callback is yet to be invoked, then we say that the Promise is pending
- **Settled**: A Promise is said to be settled if it's either fulfilled or rejected, but not pending

Once a Promise is fulfilled or rejected, it cannot be transitioned back. An attempt to transition it will have no effect.

> If the `resolve` callback is invoked with a Promise object as an argument, then the Promise object is either fulfilled or rejected, depending on whether the passed Promise object is fulfilled or rejected.

The fulfillment value

The fulfillment value of a fulfilled Promise represents the result of a successful asynchronous operation.

If the argument that we passed to the `resolve` callback is anything other than another Promise object, then the argument itself is considered as a fulfillment value of the Promise object.

If we pass nothing to the `resolve` callback, then the fulfillment value is considered as `undefined`, and the Promise is considered to be fulfilled.

To see what happens when we pass a Promise object as an argument to the `resolve` callback, consider this example—suppose we have a Promise named A. Promise A's `resolve` callback was called by passing Promise B as argument then Promise A is said to be fulfilled if Promise B is fulfilled and the fulfillment value of Promise A now is same as the fulfillment value of Promise B.

Consider this code example:

```
var a = new Promise(function(resolve, reject){
  var b = new Promise(function(res, rej){
    rej("Reason");
  });

  resolve(b);
});

var c = new Promise(function(resolve, reject){
  var d = new Promise(function(res, rej){
    res("Result");
  });

  resolve(d);
});
```

In the previous example, as Promise B gets rejected, therefore Promise A also gets rejected. The reason for the rejection of both the Promises is the string called `"Reason"`. Similarly, C gets fulfilled if D gets fulfilled. The fulfillment value of C and D is the string called `"Result"`.

> When we say that "a Promise resolves with a value, or is resolved with a value," it means that the executor of the Promise invokes or has invoked the `resolve` callback with the value.

The then(onFulfilled, onRejected) method

The `then()` method of a Promise object lets us do some task after a Promise has been fulfilled or rejected. The task can also be another event-driven or callback-based asynchronous operation.

The `then()` method of a Promise object takes two arguments, that is, the `onFulfilled` and `onRejected` callbacks. The `onFulfilled` callback is executed if the Promise object was fulfilled, and the `onRejected` callback is executed if the Promise was rejected.

The `onRejected` callback is also executed if an exception is thrown in the scope of the executor. Therefore, it behaves like an exception handler, that is, it catches the exceptions.

The `onFulfilled` callback takes a parameter, that is, the fulfillment value of the Promise. Similarly, the `onRejected` callback takes a parameter, that is, the reason of rejection.

Asynchronous Programming

The callbacks passed to the `then()` method are executed asynchronously.

Here is the code example to demonstrate the `then()` method:

```
var promise = new Promise(function(resolve, reject){
  var request = new XMLHttpRequest();
  var url = "data.json";
  request.open("GET", url);
  request.addEventListener("load", function(){
    if(request.status === 200)
    {
      resolve(request.responseText);
    }
    else
    {
      reject("Server Error: " + request.status);
    }
  }, false);
  request.addEventListener("error", function(){
    reject("Cannot Make AJAX Request");
  }, false);

  request.send();
});

promise.then(function(value){
  value = JSON.parse(value);
  return value;
}, function(reason){
  console.log(reason);
});
```

Here, if the AJAX request was successful (that is, the Promise was fulfilled), then the `onFulfilled` callback is executed by passing the response text as the argument. The `onFulfilled` callback converts the JSON string into the JavaScript object. The `onFulfilled` callback returns the JavaScript object.

Many programmers remove the Promise object variable, and write the preceding code in this way:

```
function ajax()
{
  return new Promise(function(resolve, reject){
    var request = new XMLHttpRequest();
    var url = "data.json";
```

```
      request.open("GET", url);
      request.addEventListener("load", function(){
        if(request.status === 200)
        {
          resolve(request.responseText);
        }
        else
        {
          reject("Server Error: " + request.status);
        }
      }, false);
      request.addEventListener("error", function(){
        reject("Cannot Make AJAX Request");
      }, false);

      request.send();
    });
  }

  ajax().then(function(value){
    value = JSON.parse(value);
    return value;
  }, function(reason){
    console.log(reason);
  });
```

This style makes the code even easier to read. All the new JavaScript APIs that are implemented using Promises come in this pattern.

The `then()` method always returns a new `promise` object, which resolves the return value of the calling callback. Here is how a new `promise` object is returned by the `then()` method:

- If the `onFulfilled` callback is called and there is no return statement in it, then a new fulfilled Promise is created internally and returned.
- If the `onFulfilled` callback is called and we return a custom Promise, then it internally creates and returns a new `promise` object. The new Promise object resolves the custom Promise object.
- If the `onFulfilled` callback is called and we return something else other than a custom Promise, then also a new Promise object is created internally and returned. The new Promise object resolves the return value.

Asynchronous Programming

- If we pass `null` instead of the `onFulfilled` callback, then a callback is created internally and replaced with the `null`. The internally created `onFulfilled` returns a new fulfilled `promise` object. The fulfillment value of the new `promise` object is same as the fulfillment value of the parent Promise.
- If the `onRejected` callback is called and there is no return statement in it, then a new rejected Promise is created internally and returned.
- If `onRejected` callback is called and we return a custom Promise, then it internally creates and returns a new `promise` object. The new `promise` object resolves the custom `promise` object.
- If the `onRejected` callback is called and we return something else other than a custom Promise, then also a new `promise` object is created internally and returned. The new `promise` object resolves the returned value.
- If we pass `null` instead of the `onRejected` callback, or omit it, then a callback is created internally and is used instead. The internally created `onRejected` callback returns a new rejected `promise` object. The reason of rejection of the new `promise` object is same as the reason of rejection of the parent Promise.

In the previous code example, we haven't yet logged the retrieved data to console. We can chain Promises to do this. And also in the previous code, we do not handle the exceptions that might occur in the `onFulfilled` callback. Here is how we can expand the code to log data and also handle exceptions of all the `onFulfilled` callbacks chained:

```
function ajax()
{
  return new Promise(function(resolve, reject){
    var request = new XMLHttpRequest();
    var url = "data.json";
    request.open("GET", url);
    request.addEventListener("load", function(){
      if(request.status === 200)
      {
        resolve(request.responseText);
      }
      else
      {
        reject("Server Error: " + request.status);
      }
    }, false);
    request.addEventListener("error", function(){
      reject("Cannot Make AJAX Request");
```

```
    }, false);

    request.send();
  });
}

ajax().then(function(value){
  value = JSON.parse(value);
  return value;
}).then(function(value){
  console.log(value.Name);
  return value;
}).then(function(value){
  console.log(value.Profession);
  return value;
}).then(function(value){
  console.log(value.Age);
  return value;
}).then(null, function(reason){
  console.log(reason);
});
```

In this code example, we chained multiple Promises using the `then()` method to parse and log the response received by the executor of the first Promise of the chain. Here, the last `then()` method is used as an exception or error handler for all the `onFulfilled` methods and executors.

Here is an image that shows how the execution of multiple chained Promises work:

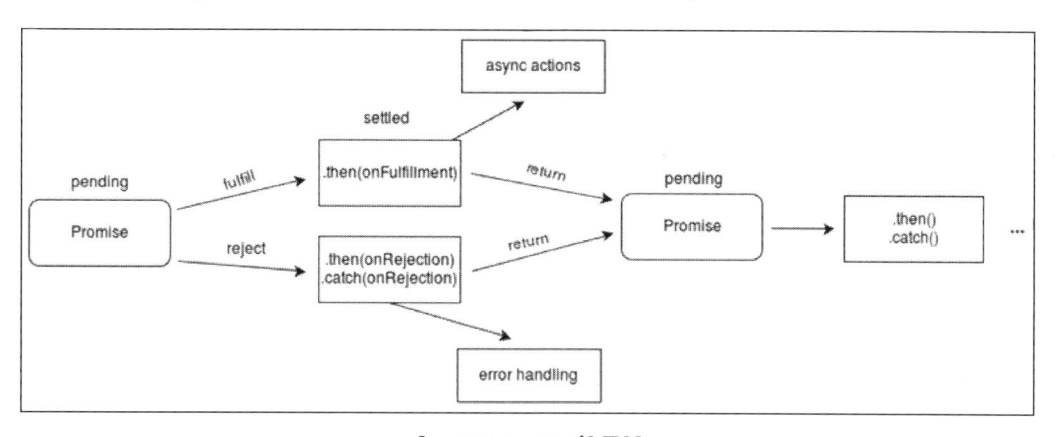

Image courtesy of MDN

Asynchronous Programming

Let's go ahead and add an event driven asynchronous operation to the chain, that is, to verify if the data displayed is correct or not. Here is how we can expand the code to do this:

```
function ajax()
{
   return new Promise(function(resolve, reject){
      var request = new XMLHttpRequest();
      var url = "http://localhost:8888/data.json";
      request.open("GET", url);
      request.addEventListener("load", function(){
         if(request.status === 200)
         {
            resolve(request.responseText);
         }
         else
         {
            reject("Server Error: " + request.status);
         }
      }, false);
      request.addEventListener("error", function(){
         reject("Cannot Make AJAX Request");
      }, false);

      request.send();
   });
}

function verify(value)
{
   return new Promise(function(resolve, reject){
      if(value == true)
      {
         //make AJAX request to send data to server
      }
      else
      {
         //make AJAX request to send data to server
      }
   });
}

ajax().then(function(value){
   value = JSON.parse(value);
```

```
      return value;
  }).then(function(value){
    console.log(value.Name);
    return value;
  }).then(function(value){
    console.log(value.Profession);
    return value;
  }).then(function(value){
    console.log(value.Age);
    return value;
  }).then(function(value){
    var result = confirm("Is the data correct?");
    return result;
  }).then(verify).then(null, function(reason){
    console.log(reason);
  });
```

Now we can see how wrapping the AJAX operation with Promises made the code easier to read and write. Now the code is more understandable at first glance.

The catch(onRejected) method

The `catch()` method of a `promise` object is used instead of the `then()` method, when we use the `then()` method only to handle errors and exceptions. There is nothing special about how the `catch()` method works. It's just that it makes the code much easier to read, as the word "catch" makes it more meaningful.

The `catch()` method just takes one argument, that is, the `onRejected` callback. The `onRejected` callback of the `catch()` method is invoked in the same way as the `onRejected` callback of the `then()` method.

The `catch()` method always returns a Promise. Here is how a new `promise` object is returned by the `catch()` method:

- If there is no return statement in the `onRejected` callback, then a new fulfilled Promise is created internally and returned.
- If we return a custom Promise, then it internally creates and returns a new `promise` object. The new `promise` object resolves the custom `promise` object.
- If we return something else other than a custom Promise in the `onRejected` callback, then also a new `promise` object is created internally and returned. The new `promise` object resolves the returned value.

- If we pass `null` instead of the `onRejected` callback, or omit it, then a callback is created internally and used instead. The internally created `onRejected` callback returns a rejected `promise` object. The reason for the rejection of the new `promise` object is same as the reason for the rejection of a parent `promise` object.
- If the `promise` object to which `catch()` is called gets fulfilled, then the `catch()` method simply returns a new fulfilled `promise` object and ignores the `onRejected` callback. The fulfillment value of the new `promise` object is same as the fulfillment value of the parent Promise.

To understand the `catch()` method, consider this code:

```
promise.then(null, function(reason){
});
```

This code can be rewritten in this way using the `catch()` method:

```
promise.catch(function(reason){
});
```

These two code snippets work exactly in the same way.

Let's rewrite the AJAX code example by replacing the last chained `then()` method with the `catch()` method:

```
function ajax()
{
  return new Promise(function(resolve, reject){
    var request = new XMLHttpRequest();
    var url = "data.json";
    request.open("GET", url);
    request.addEventListener("load", function(){
      if(request.status === 200)
      {
        resolve(request.responseText);
      }
      else
      {
        reject("Server Error: " + request.status);
      }
    }, false);
    request.addEventListener("error", function(){
      reject("Cannot Make AJAX Request");
    }, false);
```

```
      request.send();
    });
  }

  function verify(value)
  {
    return new Promise(function(resolve, reject){
      if(value == true)
      {
        //make AJAX request to send data to server
      }
      else
      {
        //make AJAX request to send data to server
      }
    });
  }

  ajax().then(function(value){
    value = JSON.parse(value);
    return value;
  }).then(function(value){
    console.log(value.Name);
    return value;
  }).then(function(value){
    console.log(value.Profession);
    return value;
  }).then(function(value){
    console.log(value.Age);
    return value;
  }).then(function(value){
    var result = confirm("Is the data correct?");
    return result;
  }).then(verify)
  .catch(function(reason){
    console.log(reason);
  });
```

Now the code is even easier to read at first glance.

Asynchronous Programming

The Promise.resolve(value) method

The `resolve()` method of the `Promise` object takes a value and returns a `promise` object that resolves the passed value.

The `resolve()` method is basically used to convert a value to an `promise` object. It is useful when you find yourself with a value that may or may not be a Promise, but you want to use it as a Promise. For example, the jQuery Promises have different interfaces than the ES6 Promises. Therefore, you can use the `resolve()` method to convert the jQuery Promises into the ES6 Promises.

Here is code example that demonstrates how to use the `resolve()` method:

```
var p1 = Promise.resolve(4);
p1.then(function(value){
  console.log(value);
});

//passed a promise object
Promise.resolve(p1).then(function(value){
  console.log(value);
});

Promise.resolve({name: "Eden"}).then(function(value){
  console.log(value.name);
});
```

The output is as follows:

```
4
4
Eden
```

The Promise.reject(value) method

The `reject()` method of the `Promise` object takes a value and returns a rejected `promise` object with the passed value as the reason.

Unlike `Promise.resolve()` method, the `reject()` method is used for debugging purposes and not for converting values into Promises.

Here is code example that demonstrates how to use the `reject()` method:

```
var p1 = Promise.reject(4);
p1.then(null, function(value){
  console.log(value);
```

[94]

```
});

Promise.reject({name: "Eden"}).then(null, function(value){
  console.log(value.name);
});
```

The output is as follows:

```
4
Eden
```

The Promise.all(iterable) method

The `all()` method of the `Promise` object takes an iterable object as an argument and returns a Promise that fulfills when all of the Promises in the iterable object have been fulfilled.

This can be useful when we want to execute some task after some asynchronous operations have finished.

Here is code example which demonstrates how to use the `Promise.all()` method:

```
var p1 = new Promise(function(resolve, reject){
  setTimeout(function(){
    resolve();
  }, 1000);
});

var p2 = new Promise(function(resolve, reject){
  setTimeout(function(){
    resolve();
  }, 2000);
});

var arr = [p1, p2];

Promise.all(arr).then(function(){
  console.log("Done"); //"Done" is logged after 2 seconds
});
```

If the iterable object contains a value that is not a `promise` object, then it's converted to the Promise object using the `Promise.resolve()` method.

Asynchronous Programming

In case any of the passed Promises get rejected, then the `Promise.all()` method immediately returns a new rejected Promise for the same reason as the rejected passed Promise. Here is an example to demonstrate this:

```
var p1 = new Promise(function(resolve, reject){
  setTimeout(function(){
     reject("Error");
  }, 1000);
});

var p2 = new Promise(function(resolve, reject){
  setTimeout(function(){
     resolve();
  }, 2000);
});

var arr = [p1, p2];

Promise.all(arr).then(null, function(reason){
  console.log(reason); //"Error" is logged after 1 second
});
```

The Promise.race(iterable) method

The the `race()` method of the `Promise` object takes an iterable object as the argument and returns a Promise that fulfills or rejects as soon as one of the Promises in the iterable object is fulfilled or rejected, with the fulfillment value or reason from that Promise.

As the name suggests, the `race()` method is used to race between Promises and see which one finishes first.

Here is code example that shows how to use the `race()` method:

```
var p1 = new Promise(function(resolve, reject){
  setTimeout(function(){
     resolve("Fulfillment Value 1");
  }, 1000);
});

var p2 = new Promise(function(resolve, reject){
  setTimeout(function(){
```

```
    resolve("fulfillment Value 2");
  }, 2000);
});

var arr = [p1, p2];

Promise.race(arr).then(function(value){
  console.log(value); //Output "Fulfillment value 1"
}, function(reason){
  console.log(reason);
});
```

The JavaScript APIs based on Promises

The new asynchronous JavaScript APIs are now based on the Promise pattern instead of events and callbacks. And the new versions of the old JavaScript APIs are now based on Promises.

For example, the old version of the Battery status API and the Web Cryptography API were based on event, but the new versions of these APIs are purely implemented using Promises. Let's see an overview of these APIs.

The Battery Status API

The Battery Status API provides us the battery's current charge level and charging status. Here is a code example of the new Battery Status API:

```
navigator.getBattery().then(function(value){
  console.log("Batter Level: " + (value.level * 100));
}, function(reason){
  console.log("Error: " + reason);
});
```

The `getBattery()` method of the `navigator` object returns a fulfilled Promise if it has successfully retrieved the battery information. Otherwise, it returns a rejected Promise.

If the Promise is fulfilled, then the fulfillment value is an object holding the battery information. The `level` property of the fulfillment value represents the level of charge remaining.

The Web Cryptography API

The Web Cryptography API lets us do hashing, signature generation and verification, encryption and decryption.

Here is a code example of the new Web Cryptography API:

```javascript
function convertStringToArrayBufferView(str)
{
    var bytes = new Uint8Array(str.length);
    for (var iii = 0; iii < str.length; iii++)
    {
        bytes[iii] = str.charCodeAt(iii);
    }

    return bytes;
}

function convertArrayBufferToHexaDecimal(buffer)
{
    var data_view = new DataView(buffer)
    var iii, len, hex = '', c;

    for(iii = 0, len = data_view.byteLength; iii < len; iii++)
    {
        c = data_view.getUint8(iii).toString(16);
        if(c.length < 2)
        {
            c = '0' + c;
        }

        hex += c;
    }

    return hex;
}


window.crypto.subtle.digest({name: "SHA-256"}, convertStringToArrayBufferView("ECMAScript 6")).then(function(result){
  var hash_value = convertArrayBufferToHexaDecimal(result);
  console.log(hash_value);
});
```

In this code example, we will find the SHA-256 hash value of a string.

The `window.crypto.subtle.digest` method takes an array buffer of a string and hash the algorithm name, and returns a Promise object. If it has successfully produced the hashes value, then it returns a fulfilled Promise and the fulfillment value is an array buffer representing the hash value.

Summary

In this chapter, we learned how JavaScript executes the asynchronous code. We learned about the different patterns of writing asynchronous code. We saw how Promises make it easier to read and write the asynchronous code, and how to use the ES6 Promise API. We also saw some JavaScript APIs that are based on Promises. Overall, the chapter aimed at explaining Promises, their benefits, and how to use APIs that are based on them.

In the next chapter, we will learn about ES6 Reflect API and its uses.

5
Implementing the Reflect API

ES6 introduced a new API, the **Reflect API** for the object reflection (that is, inspecting and manipulating the properties of objects). Although ES5 already had APIs for the object reflection, these APIs were not well organized and on failure, they used to throw exception. The ES6 Reflect API is well organized and makes it easier to read and write code, as it doesn't throw exceptions on failure. Instead, it returns the Boolean value, representing if the operation was true or false. Since developers are adapting to the Reflect API for the object reflection, it's important to learn this API in depth.

In this chapter, we'll cover:

- Calling a function with a given `this` value
- Invoking a constructor with the `prototype` property of another constructor
- Defining or modifying the attributes of the object properties
- Enumerating over the properties of an object using an iterator object
- Retrieving and setting the internal `[[prototype]]` property of an object
- And a lot of other operations related to inspecting and manipulating methods and properties of objects.

The Reflect object

The ES6 global `Reflect` object exposes all the new methods for the object reflection. `Reflect` is not a function object therefore, you cannot invoke the `Reflect` object. Also, you cannot use it with the `new` operator.

All the methods of the ES6 Reflect API are wrapped in the `Reflect` object to make it look well organized.

Implementing the Reflect API

The `Reflect` object provides many methods, which overlaps the global `Object` object's methods in terms of functionality.

Let's see the various methods provided by the `Reflect` object for object reflection.

The Reflect.apply(function, this, args) method

The `Reflect.apply()` method is used to invoke a function with a given `this` value. The function invoked by `Reflect.apply()` is called as the target function. It's same as the `apply()` method of the function object.

The `Reflect.apply()` method takes three arguments:

- The first argument represents the target function.
- The second argument represents the value of this inside the target function. This argument is optional.
- The third argument is an array object, specifying the arguments of the target function. This argument is optional.

The `Reflect.apply()` method returns whatever the target function returns.

Here is code example to demonstrate how to use the `Reflect.apply()` method:

```
function function_name(a, b, c)
{
  return this.value + a + b + c;
}

var returned_value = Reflect.apply(function_name, {value: 100}, [10, 20, 30]);

console.log(returned_value); //Output "160"
```

The Reflect.construct(constructor, args, prototype) method

The `Reflect.construct()` method is used to invoke a function as a constructor. It's similar to the `new` operator. The function that will be invoked as a constructor is called as the **target constructor**.

One special reason why you may want to use the `Reflect.construct()` method instead of `new` operator is when you want the target the constructor's `prototype` to match the `prototype` an another constructor.

The Reflect.construct() method takes three arguments:

- The first argument is the target constructor.
- The second argument is an array, specifying the arguments of the target constructor. This argument is optional.
- The third argument is another constructor whose prototype will be used as the prototype of the target constructor. This argument is optional.

The Reflect.construct() method returns the new instance created by the target constructor.

Here is the code example, to demonstrate how to use the Reflect.constructor() method:

```
function constructor1(a, b)
{
  this.a = a;
  this.b = b;

  this.f = function(){
    return this.a + this.b + this.c;
  }
}

function constructor2(){}
constructor2.prototype.c = 100;

var myObject = Reflect.construct(constructor1, [1,2],
constructor2);

console.log(myObject.f()); //Output "103"
```

In the preceding example, we used the prototype of consturctor2 as the prototype of constructor1 while invoking constructor1.

The Reflect.defineProperty(object, property, descriptor) method

The Reflect.defineProperty() method defines a new property directly on an object, or modifies an existing property on an object. It returns a Boolean value indicating whether the operation was successful or not.

Implementing the Reflect API

It's similar to the `Object.defineProperty()` method. The difference is that the `Reflect.defineProperty()` method returns a Boolean, whereas the `Object.defineProperty()` returns the modified object. If the `Object.defineProperty()` method fails to modify or define an object property, then it throws exception, whereas the `Reflect.defineProperty()` method returns `false` result.

The `Reflect.defineProperty()` method takes in three arguments:

- The first argument is the object that is used to define or modify a property
- The second argument is the symbol or name of the property that is to be defined or modified
- The third argument is the descriptor for the property that being defined or modified

Understanding the data properties and accessor properties

Since ES5, every object property is either a data property or an accessor property. A data property has a value, which may or may not be writable, whereas an accessor property has getter-setter pair of functions to set and retrieve the property value.

The attributes of a data property are value, writable, enumerable, and configurable. On the other hand, the attributes of an accessor property are `set`, `get`, `enumerable`, and `configurable`.

A **descriptor** is an object that describes the attributes of a property. When creating a property using the `Reflect.defineProperty()` method, the `Object.defineProperty()` method, the `Object.defineProperties()` method, or the `Object.create()` method, we need to pass a descriptor for the property.

A data property's descriptor object has the following properties:

- **Value**: This is the value associated with the property. The default value is `undefined`.
- **Writable**: If this is `true`, then the property value can be changed with an assignment operator. The default value is `false`.
- **Configurable**: If this is `true`, then the property attributes can be changed, and the property may be deleted. The default value is `false`. Remember that when the configurable attribute is `false` and writable is `true`, the value and the writable attributes can be changed.
- **Enumerable**: If this is `true`, then the property shows up in the `for...in` loop and the `Object.keys()` method. The default value is `false`.

An accessor property's descriptor has the following properties:

- **Get**: This is a function that returns the property value. The function has no parameters and default value is undefined.
- **Set**: This is a function that sets the property value. The function will receive the new value that is being assigned to the property.
- **Configurable**: If this is true, then the property descriptor can be changed and the property may be deleted. The default value is false.
- **enumerable**: If this is true, then the property shows up in for...in loop and the Object.keys() method. The default value is false.

Depending on the properties of the descriptor object, JavaScript decides whether the property is a data property or an accessor property.

If you add a property without using the Reflect.defineProperty() method, the Object.defineProperty() method, the Object.defineProperties() method, or the Object.create() method, then the property is a data property and the writable, enumerable, and the configurable attributes are all set to true. After the property is added, you can modify its attributes.

If an object already has a property with the specified name while calling the Reflect.defineProperty() method, the Object.defineProperty() method or the Object.defineProperties() method, then the property is modified. The attributes that are not specified in the descriptor remain the same.

You can change a data property to an accessor property, and vice-versa. If you do this, the configurable and the enumerable attributes that are not specified in the descriptor will be preserved in the property. Other attributes that are not specified in the descriptor are set to their default values.

Here is an example code that demonstrates how to create a data property using the Reflect.defineProperty() method:

```
var obj = {}

Reflect.defineProperty(obj, "name", {
  value: "Eden",
  writable: true,
  configurable: true,
  enumerable: true
});

console.log(obj.name); //Output "Eden"
```

Here is another example code that demonstrates how to create a accessor property using the `Reflect.defineProperty()` method:

```
var obj = {
   __name__: "Eden"
}

Reflect.defineProperty(obj, "name", {
  get: function(){
    return this.__name__;
  },
  set: function(newName){
    this.__name__ = newName;
  },
  configurable: true,
  enumerable: true
});

obj.name = "John";
console.log(obj.name);       //Output "John"
```

The Reflect.deleteProperty(object, property) method

The `Reflect.deleteProperty()` method is used to delete a property of an object. It's the same as the `delete` operator.

This method takes two arguments, that is, the first argument is the reference to the object and the second argument is the name of the property to delete. The `Reflect.deleteProperty()` method returns `true` if it has deleted the property successfully. Otherwise, it returns `false`.

Here is code example that demonstrates how to delete a property using the `Reflect.deleteProperty()` method:

```
var obj = {
  name: "Eden"
}

console.log(obj.name);       //Output "Eden"

Reflect.deleteProperty(obj, "name");

console.log(obj.name);       //Output "undefined"
```

The Reflect.enumerate(object) method

The `Reflect.enumerate()` method takes an object as argument and returns an iterator object that represents the enumerable properties of the object. It also returns the enumerable inherited properties of an object.

The `Reflect.enumerate()` method is similar to the `for...in` loop. The `Reflect.enumerate()` method returns an iterator, whereas the `for...in` loop iterates over enumerable properties.

Here is an example to demonstrate how to use the `Reflect.enumerate()` method:

```
var obj = {
  a: 1,
  b: 2,
  c: 3
};

var iterator = Reflect.enumerate(obj);

console.log(iterator.next().value);
console.log(iterator.next().value);
console.log(iterator.next().value);
console.log(iterator.next().done);
```

The output is as follows:

```
a
b
c
true
```

The Reflect.get(object, property, this) method

The `Reflect.get()` method is used to retrieve the value of an object's property. The first argument is the object and the second argument is the property name. If the property is an accessor property, then we can provide a third argument which will be the value of `this` inside the `get` function.

Here is code example that demonstrates how to use the `Reflect.get()` method:

```
var obj = {
  __name__: "Eden"
};
```

```
Reflect.defineProperty(obj, "name", {
  get: function(){
    return this.__name__;
  }
});

console.log(obj.name);       //Output "Eden"

var name = Reflect.get(obj, "name", {__name__: "John"});

console.log(name);       //Output "John"
```

The Reflect.set(object, property, value, this) method

The `Reflect.set()` method is used to set the value of an object's property. The first argument is the object, the second argument is the property name, and the third argument is the property value. If the property is an accessor property, then we can provide a fourth argument which will be the value of `this` inside the set function.

The `Reflect.set()` method returns `true` if the property value was set successfully. Otherwise, it returns `false`.

Here is code example that demonstrates how to use the `Reflect.set()` method:

```
var obj1 = {
  __name__: "Eden"
};

Reflect.defineProperty(obj1, "name", {
  set: function(newName){
    this.__name__ = newName;
  },

  get: function(){
    return this.__name__;
  }
});

var obj2 = {
  __name__: "John"
};
```

```
Reflect.set(obj1, "name", "Eden", obj2);

console.log(obj1.name); //Output "Eden"
console.log(obj2.__name__); //Output "Eden"
```

The Reflect.getOwnPropertyDescriptor(object, property) method

The `Reflect.getOwnPropertyDescriptor()` method is used to retrieve the descriptor of an object's property.

The `Reflect.getOwnPropertyDescriptor()` method is same as the `Object.getOwnPropertyDescriptor()` method. The `Reflect.getOwnPropertyDescriptor()` method takes two arguments. The first argument is the object and the second argument is the property name.

Here is an example to demonstrate the `Reflect.getOwnPropertyDescriptor()` method:

```
var obj = {
  name: "Eden"
};

var descriptor = Reflect.getOwnPropertyDescriptor(obj, "name");

console.log(descriptor.value);
console.log(descriptor.writable);
console.log(descriptor.enumerable);
console.log(descriptor.configurable);
```

The output is as the following:

```
Eden
true
true
true
```

The Reflect.getPrototypeOf(object) method

The `Reflect.getPrototypeOf()` method is used to retrieve prototype of an object that is, the value of the internal `[[prototype]]` property of an object.

The `Reflect.getPrototypeOf()` method is same as the `Object.getPrototypeOf()` method.

Implementing the Reflect API

Here is the code example that demonstrates how to use the `Reflect.getPrototypeOf()` method:

```
var obj1 = {
  __proto__: {
    name: "Eden"
  }
};

var obj2 = Reflect.getPrototypeOf(obj1);

console.log(obj2.name); //Output "Eden"
```

The Reflect.setPrototypeOf(object, prototype) method

The `Reflect.setPrototypeOf()` is used to set the internal `[[prototype]]` property's value of an object. The `Reflect.setPrototypeOf()` method will return `true` if the internal `[[prototype]]` property's value was set successfully. Otherwise, it will return `false`.

Here is a code example, which demonstrates how to use it:

```
var obj = {};

Reflect.setPrototypeOf(obj, {
  name: "Eden"
});

console.log(obj.name); //Output "Eden"
```

The Reflect.has(object, property) method

The `Reflect.has()` is used to check if a property exists in an object. It also checks for the inherited properties. It returns `true` if the property exists. Otherwise it'd return as `false`.

It's same as the `in` operator.

Here is code example that demonstrates how to use the `Reflect.has()` method:

```
var obj = {
  __proto__: {
    name: "Eden"
```

```
  },
  age: 12
};

console.log(Reflect.has(obj, "name")); //Output "true"
console.log(Reflect.has(obj, "age")); //Output "true"
```

The Reflect.isExtensible(object) method

The `Reflect.isExtensible()` method is used to check if an object is extensible or not, that is, if we can add new properties to an object.

An object can be marked as non-extensible using the `Object.preventExtensions()`, `Object.freeze()` and the `Object.seal()` methods.

The `Reflect.isExtensible()` method is same as the `Object.isExtensible()` method.

Here is code example, which demonstrates how to use the `Reflect.isExtensible()` method:

```
var obj = {
  name: "Eden"
};

console.log(Reflect.isExtensible(obj)); //Output "true"

Object.preventExtensions(obj);

console.log(Reflect.isExtensible(obj)); //Output "false"
```

The Reflect.preventExtensions(object) method

The `Reflect.preventExtensions()` is used to mark an object as non-extensible. It returns a Boolean, indicating whether the operation was successful or not.

It's same as the `Object.preventExtensions()` method:

```
var obj = {
  name: "Eden"
};
```

```
console.log(Reflect.isExtensible(obj)); //Output "true"

console.log(Reflect.preventExtensions(obj)); //Output "true"

console.log(Reflect.isExtensible(obj)); //Output "false"
```

The Reflect.ownKeys(object) method

The `Reflect.ownKeys()` method returns an array whose values represent the keys of the properties of an provided object. It ignores the inherited properties.

Here is the example code to demonstrate this method:

```
var obj = {
  a: 1,
  b: 2,
  __proto__: {
    c: 3
  }
};

var keys = Reflect.ownKeys(obj);

console.log(keys.length); //Output "2"
console.log(keys[0]); //Output "a"
console.log(keys[1]); //Output "b"
```

Summary

In this chapter, we learned what the object reflection is, and how to use the ES6 Reflect API for the object reflection. We saw various methods of the `Reflect` object with examples. Overall, this chapter introduced the ES6 Reflect API to inspect and manipulate the properties of objects.

In the next chapter, we will learn about the ES6 proxies and their uses.

6
Using Proxies

Proxies are used to define the custom behavior for the fundamental operations on objects. Proxies are already available in the programming languages such as C#, C++, and Java, but JavaScript has never had proxies. ES6 introduced the Proxy API, which lets us create proxies. In this chapter, we will look at proxies, their usage, and the proxy traps. Due to the benefits of proxies, the developers are using proxies increasingly and therefore, it's important to learn about proxies in-depth with examples, which we will do in this chapter.

In this chapter, we'll cover:

- Creating proxies using the Proxy API
- Understanding what proxies are and how to use them
- Intercepting various operations on the objects using traps
- The different kinds of available traps
- Some use cases of proxies

Proxies in a nutshell

A proxy acts like a wrapper for an object, and defines the custom behavior for the fundamental operations on the object. Some fundamental operations on the objects are property lookup, property assignment, constructor invocation, enumeration, and so on.

Once an object is wrapped using a proxy, all the operations that are supposed to be done on the object should now be done on the proxy object, so that the custom behavior can take place.

Terminology

Here are some important terms that are used while studying proxies:

- Target: This is the object that is wrapped by proxy.
- Traps: These are functions that intercept various operations on the target object, and define the custom behavior for those operations.
- Handler: This is an object that holds the traps. A handler is attached to a proxy object.

The Proxy API

The ES6 Proxy API provides the `Proxy` constructor to create proxies. The `Proxy` constructor takes two arguments, which are:

- **Target**: This is the object that will be wrapped by the proxy
- **Handler**: This is an object that contains the traps for the target object

A trap can be defined for every possible operation on the target object. If a trap is not defined, then the default action takes place on the target.

Here is a code example that shows how to create a proxy, and do various operations on the target object. In this example, we have not defined any traps:

```
var target = {
  age: 12
};
var handler = {};
var proxy = new Proxy(target, handler);

proxy.name = "Eden";

console.log(target.name);
console.log(proxy.name);
console.log(target.age);
console.log(proxy.age);
```

The output is as follows:

```
Eden
Eden
12
12
```

Here, we can see that the age property of the target object can be accessed via the proxy object. And when we added the name property to the proxy object, it was actually added to the target object.

As there was no trap attached for the property assignment, the proxy.name assignment resulted to the default behavior that is simply assigning the value to the property.

So, we can say a proxy is just a wrapper for a target object and traps can be defined to change the default behavior of operations.

Many developers don't keep a reference variable for the target object to make use of the proxy mandatory for accessing the object. Keep a reference for the handler only when you need to reuse it for multiple proxies. Here is how they rewrite the previous code:

```
var proxy = new Proxy({
  age: 12
}, {});

proxy.name = "Eden";
```

Traps

There are different traps for different operations that can be performed on an object. Some of the traps need to return values. There are some rules they need to follow while returning values. The returned values are intercepted by the proxy to filter, and/or to check if the returned values obey the rules. If a trap doesn't obey rules while returning value, then the proxy throws the TypeError exception.

The value of this inside a trap is always a reference to the handler.

Lets take a look at the various kinds of traps.

The get(target, property, receiver) method

The get trap is executed when we retrieve a property value using the dot or bracket notation, or the Reflect.get() method. It takes three parameters, that is, the target object, the property name, and the proxy.

It must return a value that represens the property value.

Using Proxies

Here is a code example, which shows how to use the `get` trap:

```
var proxy = new Proxy({
    age: 12
}, {
    get: function(target, property, receiver){
      if(property in target)
      {
        return target[property];
      }
      else
      {
        return "Not Found";
      }
    }
  }
);

console.log(Reflect.get(proxy, "age"));
console.log(Reflect.get(proxy, "name"));
```

The output is as follows:

```
12
Not found
```

Here, we can see that the `get` trap looks for the property in the `target` object, and if it finds it, then returns the property value. Otherwise, it returns a string indicating that it was not found.

The `receiver` parameter is the reference of the object whose property we intended to access. Consider this example to better understand the value of the `receiver` parameter:

```
var proxy = new Proxy({age: 13}, {
    get: function(target, property, receiver){

      console.log(receiver);

      if(property in target)
      {
        console.log(receiver);
        return target[property];
      }
```

```
      else
      {
        return "Not Found";
      }
    }
  }
);

var temp = proxy.name;

var obj = {
  age: 12,
  __proto__: proxy
}

temp = obj.name;
```

The output is as follows:

```
{age: 13}
{age: 12}
```

Here `obj` inherits the `proxy` object. Therefore, when the `name` property was not found in the `obj` object, it was looked in the `proxy` object. As the `proxy` object had a `get` trap, it provided a value.

So, the value of the `receiver` parameter when we accessed the `name` property via the `obj.name` expression, is `obj`, and when we accessed the `name` property via `proxy.name` expression is `proxy`.

The value of the `receiver` parameter is decided in the same way for all other traps also.

Rules

These rules shouldn't be violated while using the `get` trap:

- The value returned for a property must be the same as the value of the target object property if the target object property is a non-writable, non-configurable data property.
- The value returned for a property must be `undefined` if the target object property is non-configurable accessor property that has `undefined` as its `[[Get]]` attribute.

The set(target, property, value, receiver) method

The `set` trap is invoked when we set the value of a property using the assignment operator, or the `Reflect.set()` method. It takes four parameters, that is, the target object, the property name, the new property value, and the receiver.

The `set` trap must return `true` if the assignment was successful. Otherwise, it will return `false`.

Here is a code example, which demonstrates how to use the `set` trap:

```
var proxy = new Proxy({}, {
  set: function(target, property, value, receiver){
    target[property] = value;
    return true;
  }
});

Reflect.set(proxy, "name", "Eden");
console.log(proxy.name); //Output "Eden"
```

Rules

These rules shouldn't be violated while using the `set` trap:

- If the target object property is a non-writable, non-configurable data property, then it will return as `false`, that is, you cannot change the property value
- If the target object property is a non-configurable accessor property that has `undefined` as its `[[Set]]` attribute, then it will return as false, that is, you cannot change the property value

The has(target, property) method

The `has` trap is executed when we check if a property exists or not, using the `in` operator. It takes two parameters, that is, the target object and the property name. It must return a Boolean value that indicates whether the property exists or not.

Here is a code example, which demonstrates how to use the `has` trap:

```
var proxy = new Proxy({age: 12}, {
  has: function(target, property){
    if(property in target)
    {
      return true;
    }
```

[118]

```
      else
      {
        return false;
      }
    }
  }
});

console.log(Reflect.has(proxy, "name"));
console.log(Reflect.has(proxy, "age"));
```

The output is as follows:

```
false
true
```

Rules

These rules shouldn't be violated while using the `has` trap:

- You cannot return `false` if the property exists as a non-configurable own property of the `target` object
- You cannot return `false` if the property exists as an own property of the `target` object, and the `target` object is not extensible

The isExtensible(target) method

The `isExtensible` trap is executed when we check if the object is extensible or not, using the `Object.isExtensible()` method. It takes only one parameter, that is, the `target` object. It must return a Boolean value indicating whether the object is extensible or not.

Here is a code example, which demonstrates how to use the `isExtensible` trap:

```
var proxy = new Proxy({age: 12}, {
  isExtensible: function(target){
    return Object.isExtensible(target);
  }
});

console.log(Reflect.isExtensible(proxy)); //Output "true"
```

Rules

These rules shouldn't be violated while using the `isExtensible` trap:

- You cannot return `false` if the target is extensible. Similarly, you cannot return `true` if the target is non-extensible.

The getPrototypeOf(target) method

The `getPrototypeOf` trap is executed when we retrieve the value of the internal `[[prototype]]` property, using either the `Object.getPrototypeOf()` method or the `__proto__` property. It takes only one parameter, that is, the `target` object.

It must return an object or `null` value. The `null` value indicates that the object doesn't inherit anything else and is the end of the inheritance chain.

Here is a code example, which demonstrates how to use the `getPrototypeOf` trap:

```
var proxy = new Proxy({age: 12, __proto__: {name: "Eden"}}, {
  getPrototypeOf: function(target){
    return Object.getPrototypeOf(target);
  }
});

console.log(Reflect.getPrototypeOf(proxy).name); //Output "Eden"
```

Rules

These rules shouldn't be violated while using the `getPrototypeOf` trap:

- It must either return an object or return `null` value.
- If the target is not extensible, then this trap must return the actual prototype

The setPrototypeOf(target, prototype) method

The `setPrototypeOf` trap is executed when we set the value of the internal `[[prototype]]` property, using either the `Object.setPrototypeOf()` method or the `__proto__` property. It takes two parameters, that is, the target object and value of the property to be assigned.

This trap will return a Boolean, indicating whether it has successfully set the prototype or not.

Here is a code example, which demonstrates how to use the `setPrototypeOf` trap:

```
var proxy = new Proxy({}, {
  setPrototypeOf: function(target, value){
    Reflect.setPrototypeOf(target, value);
    return true;
  }
});

Reflect.setPrototypeOf(proxy, {name: "Eden"});

console.log(Reflect.getPrototypeOf(proxy).name); //Output "Eden"
```

Rules

These rules shouldn't be violated while using the `setPrototypeOf` trap:

- You must return `false` if the target is not extensible

The preventExtensions(target) method

The `preventExtensions` trap is executed when we prevent the addition of new properties using the `Object.preventExtensions()` method. It takes only one parameter, that is, the `target` object.

It must return a Boolean, indicating weather it has successfully prevented the extension of the object or not.

Here is a code example, which demonstrates how to use the `preventExtensions` trap:

```
var proxy = new Proxy({}, {
  preventExtensions: function(target){
    Object.preventExtensions(target);
    return true;
  }
});

Reflect.preventExtensions(proxy);

proxy.a = 12;
console.log(proxy.a); //Output "undefined"
```

Rules

These rules shouldn't be violated while using the `preventExtensions` trap:

- This trap can return `true` only if the target is non-extensible, or it has made the target non-extensible

The getOwnPropertyDescriptor(target, property) method

The `getOwnPropertyDescriptor` trap is executed when we retrieve the descriptor of a property by using the `Object.getOwnPropertyDescriptor()` method. It takes two parameters, that is, the target object and the name of the property.

This trap must return a descriptor object or `undefined`. The `undefined` value is returned if the property doesn't exist.

Here is a code example, which demonstrates how to use the `getOwnPropertyDescriptor` trap:

```
var proxy = new Proxy({age: 12}, {
  getOwnPropertyDescriptor: function(target, property){
    return Object.getOwnPropertyDescriptor(target, property);
  }
});

var descriptor = Reflect.getOwnPropertyDescriptor(proxy, "age");

console.log("Enumerable: " + descriptor.enumerable);
console.log("Writable: " + descriptor.writable);
console.log("Configurable: " + descriptor.configurable);
console.log("Value: " + descriptor.value);
```

The output is as follows:

```
Enumerable: true
Writable: true
Configurable: true
Value: 12
```

Rules

These rules shouldn't be violated while using the `getOwnPropertyDescriptor` trap:

- This trap must either return an object or return an `undefined` property
- You cannot return the `undefined` value if the property exists as a non-configurable own property of the `target` object
- You cannot return the `undefined` value if the property exists as an own property of the `target` object, and the `target` object is not extensible
- You will have to return `undefined`, if the property does not exist as an own property of the `target` object, and the `target` object is not extensible
- You cannot make the `configurable` property of the returned descriptor object false, if the property exists as an own property of the `target` object, or if it exists as a configurable own property of the `target` object

The defineProperty(target, property, descriptor) method

The `defineProperty` trap is executed when we define a property using the `Object.defineProperty()` method. It takes three parameters, that is, the `target` object, the `property` name, and the `descriptor` object.

This trap should return a Boolean indicating whether it has successfully defined the property or not.

Here is a code example, which demonstrates how to use the `defineProperty` trap:

```
var proxy = new Proxy({}, {
  defineProperty: function(target, property, descriptor){
    Object.defineProperty(target, property, descriptor);
    return true;
  }
});

Reflect.defineProperty(proxy, "name", {value: "Eden"});

console.log(proxy.name); //Output "Eden"
```

Rules

These rules shouldn't be violated while using the `defineProperty` trap:

- It must return `false` if the `target` object is not extensible, and the property doesn't yet exist

The deleteProperty(target, property) method

The `deleteProperty` trap is executed when we delete a property using either the `delete` operator or the `Reflect.deleteProperty()` method. It takes two parameters, that is, the `target` object and the `property` name.

This trap must return a Boolean, indicating whether the property was deleted successfully or not.

Here is a code example, which demonstrates how to use the `deleteProperty` trap:

```
var proxy = new Proxy({age: 12}, {
  deleteProperty: function(target, property){
      return delete target[property];
  }
});

Reflect.deleteProperty(proxy, "age");
console.log(proxy.age); //Output "undefined"
```

Rules

This rule shouldn't be violated while using the `deleteProperty` trap:

- This trap must return `false` if the property exists as a non-configurable own property of the `target` object

The enumerate(target) method

The `enumerate` trap is executed when we loop over the property keys using either the `for...in` loop or the `Reflect.enumerate()` method. It takes one parameter, that is, the `target` object.

This trap must return an iterator object, representing the enumerable keys of the object.

Here is a code example, which demonstrates how to use the `enumerate` trap:

```
var proxy = new Proxy({age: 12, name: "Eden"}, {
  enumerate: function(target){
    var arr = [];

    for(var p in target)
    {
      arr[arr.length] = p;
    }

    return arr[Symbol.iterator]();
  }
});

var iterator = Reflect.enumerate(proxy);

console.log(iterator.next().value);
console.log(iterator.next().value);
console.log(iterator.next().done);
```

Output is:

```
age
name
true
```

Rules

This rule shouldn't be violated while using the `enumerate` trap:

- This trap must return an object

The ownKeys(target) method

The `ownKeys` trap is executed when we retrieve the own property keys using the `Reflect.ownKeys()`, `Object.getOwnPropertyNames()`, `Object.getOwnPropertySymbols()`, and the `Object.keys()` methods. It takes only one parameter, that is, the `target` object.

The `Reflect.ownKeys()` method is similar to the `Object.getOwnPropertyNames()` method, that is, they return the enumerable and non-enumerable property keys of a object. They ignore the inherited properties. The only difference is that the `Reflect.ownKeys()` method returns both, the symbol and string keys, whereas the `Object.getOwnPropertyNames()` method returns only the string keys.

Using Proxies

The `Object.getOwnPropertySymbols()` method returns the enumerable and non-enumerable properties whose keys are symbols. It ignores the inherited properties.

The `Object.keys()` method is similar to the `Object.getOwnPropertyNames()` method, but the only difference is that the `Objecy.keys()` method returns the enumerable properties only.

The `ownKeys` trap must return an array, representing the own property keys.

Here is a code example, which demonstrates how to use the `ownKeys` trap:

```
var s = Symbol();

var object = {age: 12, __proto__: {name: "Eden"}, [s]: "Symbol"};

Object.defineProperty(object, "profession", {
  enumerable: false,
  configurable: false,
  writable: false,
  value: "Developer"
})

var proxy = new Proxy(object, {
  ownKeys: function(target){
     return Object.getOwnPropertyNames(target).concat(Object.getOwnPropertySymbols(target));
  }
});

console.log(Reflect.ownKeys(proxy));
console.log(Object.getOwnPropertyNames(proxy));
console.log(Object.keys(proxy));
console.log(Object.getOwnPropertySymbols(proxy));
```

The output is as follows:

```
["age", "profession", Symbol()]
["age", "profession"]
["age"]
[Symbol()]
```

Here, we can see that the values of the array returned by the `ownKeys` trap are filtered by the proxy, based on what the caller expected. For example, the `Object.getOwnPropertySymbols()` caller expected an array of symbols. Therefore, the proxy removed the strings from the returned array.

Rules

These rules shouldn't be violated while using the `ownKeys` trap:

- The elements of the returned array must either be a string or symbol
- The returned array must contain the keys of all the non-configurable own properties of the `target` object
- If the `target` object is not extensible, then the returned array must contain all the keys, of the own properties, of the `target` object, and no other values

The apply(target, thisValue, arguments) method

If the target is a function, then calling the proxy will execute the `apply` trap. The `apply` trap is also executed for function's `apply()` and `call()` methods, and the `Reflect.apply()` method.

The `apply` trap takes three parameters. The first parameter is the `target` object, and the third parameter is an array, representing the arguments of the function call. The second parameter is same as the value of `this` of the target function, that is, it's same as the value of `this` of the target function, if the target function would have been invoked without the proxy.

Here is a code example, which demonstrates how to use the `apply` trap:

```
var proxy = new Proxy(function(){}, {
  apply: function(target, thisValue, arguments){
    console.log(thisValue.name);
    return arguments[0] + arguments[1] + arguments[2];
  }
});

var obj = {
  name: "Eden",
  f: proxy
}

var sum = obj.f(1,2,3);

console.log(sum);
```

The output is as follows:

```
Eden
6
```

The construct(target, arguments) method

If the target is a function, then calling the target as a constructor using the new operator or the `Reflect.construct()` method will execute the construct trap.

The construct trap takes two parameters. The first parameter is the target object, and the second parameter is an array, representing the arguments of the constructor call.

The construct trap must return an object, representing the newly created instance.

Here is a code example, which demonstrates how to use the construct trap:

```
var proxy = new Proxy(function(){}, {
  construct: function(target, arguments){
    return {name: arguments[0]};
  }
});

var obj = new proxy("Eden");
console.log(obj.name); //Output "Eden"
```

The Proxy.revocable(target, handler) method

A revocable proxy is a proxy that can be revoked (that is, switched off).

To create the revocable, proxies we have to use the `Proxy.revocable()` method. The `Proxy.revocable()` method is not a constructor. This method also takes the same arguments as the Proxy constructor, but instead of returning a revocable proxy instance directly, it returns an object with two properties, which are the following:

- proxy: This is the revocable proxy object
- revoke: When this function is called, it revokes the proxy

Once a revocable proxy is revoked, any attempts to use it will throw a `TypeError` exception.

Here is an example to demonstrate how to create a revocable proxy and revoke it:

```
var revocableProxy = Proxy.revocable({
  age: 12
}, {
  get: function(target, property, receiver){
    if(property in target)
    {
```

```
      return target[property];
    }
    else
    {
      return "Not Found";
    }
  }
 }
);

console.log(revocableProxy.proxy.age);

revocableProxy.revoke();

console.log(revocableProxy.proxy.name);
```

The output is as follows:

```
12
TypeError: proxy is revoked
```

Use Case

You can use the revocable proxies instead of the regular proxies. You can use it when you pass a proxy to a function that runs asynchronously or is parallel so that you can revoke it anytime in case you don't want the function to be able to use that proxy anymore.

The uses of proxies

There are several uses of proxies. Here are some main use cases:

- Creating virtualized objects, such as remote objects, persistent objects, and more
- The lazy creation of objects
- Transparent logging, tracing, profiling, and more
- Embedded domain specific languages
- Generically interposing abstractions in order to enforce the access control

Summary

In this chapter, we learned what proxies are and how to use them. We saw the various traps available with examples. We also saw different rules that need to be followed by different traps. This chapter explained everything in-depth about the ES6 Proxy API. Finally, we saw some use cases of proxies.

In the next chapter, we will walk through the object oriented programming, and the ES6 classes.

7
Walking You Through Classes

ES6 introduced classes that provide a much simpler and clearer syntax to creating constructors and dealing with inheritance. JavaScript never had the concept of classes, although it's an object-oriented programming language. Programmers from the other programming language background often found it difficult to understand JavaScript's object-oriented model and inheritance due to lack of classes. In this chapter, we will learn about the object-oriented JavaScript using the ES6 classes:

- The JavaScript data types
- Creating objects the classical way
- The constructors of the primitive types
- What are classes in ES6
- Creating objects using classes
- The inheritance in classes
- The features of classes

Understanding the Object-oriented JavaScript

Before we proceed with the ES6 classes, let's refresh our knowledge on the JavaScript data types, constructors, and inheritance. While learning classes, we will be comparing the syntax of the constructors and prototype-based inheritance with the syntax of the classes. Therefore, it is important to have a good grip on these topics.

The JavaScript data types

The JavaScript variables hold (or store) data (or value). The type of data variables that they hold is called as the **data type**. In JavaScript, there are seven different data types: **number**, **string**, **Boolean**, **null**, **undefined**, **symbol**, and **object**.

When it comes to holding objects, variables hold the object reference (that is, the memory address) instead of the object itself.

All the other data types other than object are called as **primitive data types**.

> The arrays and functions are actually the JavaScript objects.

Creating objects

There are two ways of creating an object in JavaScript, that is, using the object literal, or using a constructor. The object literal is used when we want to create fixed objects, whereas constructor is used when we want to create the objects dynamically on runtime.

Let's consider a case where we may need to use the constructors instead of the object literal. Here is a code example:

```
var student = {
  name: "Eden",
  printName: function(){
    console.log(this.name);
  }
}

student.printName(); //Output "Eden"
```

Here, we created a `student` object using the object literal, that is, the {} notation. This works well when you just want to create a single `student` object.

But the problem arises when you want to create multiple `student` objects. Obviously, you don't want to write the previous code multiple times to create multiple `student` objects. This is where constructors come into use.

A function acts like a constructor when invoked using the `new` keyword. A constructor creates and returns an object. The `this` keyword, inside a function, when invoked as a constructor, points to the new object instance, and once the constructor execution is finished, the new object is automatically returned. Consider this example:

```
function Student(name)
{
  this.name = name;
}

Student.prototype.printName = function(){
  console.log(this.name);
}

var student1 = new Student("Eden");
var student2 = new Student("John");

student1.printName(); //Output "Eden"
student2.printName(); //Output "John"
```

Here, to create multiple student objects, we invoked the constructor multiple times instead of creating multiple student objects using the object literals.

To add methods to the instances of the constructor, we didn't use the `this` keyword, instead we used the `prototype` property of constructor. We will learn more on why we did it this way, and what the `prototype` property is, in the next section.

Actually, every object must belong to a constructor. Every object has an inherited property named `constructor`, pointing to the object's constructor. When we create objects using the object literal, the `constructor` property points to the global `Object` constructor. Consider this example to understand this behavior:

```
var student = {}

console.log(student.constructor == Object); //Output "true"
```

Understanding inheritance

Each JavaScript object has an internal `[[prototype]]` property pointing to another object called as its prototype. This prototype object has a prototype of its own, and so on until an object is reached with `null` as its prototype. `null` has no prototype, and it acts as a final link in the prototype chain.

Walking You Through Classes

When trying to access a property of an object, and if the property is not found in the object, then the property is searched in the object's prototype. If still not found, then it's searched in the prototype of the prototype object. It keeps on going until `null` is encountered in the prototype chain. This is how inheritance works in JavaScript.

As a JavaScript object can have only one prototype, JavaScript supports only a single inheritance.

While creating objects using the object literal, we can use the special __proto__ property or the `Object.setPrototypeOf()` method to assign a prototype of an object. JavaScript also provides an `Object.create()` method, with which we can create a new object with a specified prototype as the __proto__ lacked browser support, and the `Object.setPrototypeOf()` method seemed a little odd. Here is code example that demonstrates different ways to set the prototype of an object while creating, using the object literal:

```javascript
var object1 = {
  name: "Eden",
   __proto__: {age: 24}
}

var object2 = {name: "Eden"}
Object.setPrototypeOf(object2, {age: 24});

var object3 = Object.create({age: 24}, {name: {value: "Eden"}});

console.log(object1.name + " " + object1.age);
console.log(object2.name + " " + object2.age);
console.log(object3.name + " " + object3.age);
```

The output is as follows:

```
Eden 24
Eden 24
Eden 24
```

Here, the `{age:24}` object is referred as **base object**, **superobject**, or **parent object** as its being inherited. And the `{name:"Eden"}` object is referred as the **derived object**, **subobject**, or the **child object**, as it inherits another object.

If you don't assign a prototype to an object while creating it using the object literal, then the prototype points to the `Object.prototype` property. The prototype of `Object.prototype` is `null` therefore, leading to the end of the prototype chain. Here is an example to demonstrate this:

```
var obj = {
  name: "Eden"
}

console.log(obj.__proto__ == Object.prototype); //Output "true"
```

While creating objects using a constructor, the prototype of the new objects always points to a property named `prototype` of the function object. By default, the `prototype` property is an object with one property named as `constructor`. The `constructor` property points to the function itself. Consider this example to understand this model:

```
function Student()
{
  this.name = "Eden";
}

var obj = new Student();

console.log(obj.__proto__.constructor == Student); //Output "true"
console.log(obj.__proto__ == Student.prototype); //Output "true"
```

To add new methods to the instances of a constructor, we should add them to the `prototype` property of the constructor, as we did earlier. We shouldn't add methods using the `this` keyword in a constructor body, because every instance of the constructor will have a copy of the methods, and this isn't very memory efficient. By attaching methods to the `prototype` property of a constructor, there is only one copy of each function that all the instances share. To understand this, consider this example:

```
function Student(name)
{
    this.name = name;
}

Student.prototype.printName = function(){
    console.log(this.name);
}
```

```
var s1 = new Student("Eden");
var s2 = new Student("John");

function School(name)
{
  this.name = name;
  this.printName = function(){
    console.log(this.name);
  }
}

var s3 = new School("ABC");
var s4 = new School("XYZ");

console.log(s1.printName == s2.printName);
console.log(s3.printName == s4.printName);
```

The output is as follows:

```
true
false
```

Here, `s1` and `s2` share the same `printName` function that reduces the use of memory, whereas `s3` and `s4` contain two different functions with the name as `printName` that makes the program use more memory. This is unnecessary, as both the functions do the same thing. Therefore, we add methods for the instances to the `prototype` property of the constructor.

Implementing the inheritance hierarchy in the constructors is not as straightforward as we did for object literals. Because the child constructor needs to invoke the parent constructor for the parent constructor's initialization logic to take place and we need to add the methods of the `prototype` property of the parent constructor to the `prototype` property of the child constructor, so that we can use them with the objects of child constructor. There is no predefined way to do all this. The developers and JavaScript libraries have their own ways of doing this. I will show you the most common way of doing it.

Here is an example to demonstrate how to implement the inheritance while creating the objects using the constructors:

```
function School(schoolName)
{
  this.schoolName = schoolName;
}
School.prototype.printSchoolName = function(){
```

```
    console.log(this.schoolName);
}

function Student(studentName, schoolName)
{
  this.studentName = studentName;

  School.call(this, schoolName);
}
Student.prototype = new School();
Student.prototype.printStudentName = function(){
  console.log(this.studentName);
}

var s = new Student("Eden", "ABC School");
s.printStudentName();
s.printSchoolName();
```

The output is as follows:

```
Eden
ABC School
```

Here, we invoked the parent constructor using the `call` method of the function object. To inherit the methods, we created an instance of the parent constructor, and assigned it to the child constructor's `prototype` property.

This is not a foolproof way of implementing inheritance in the constructors, as there are lots of potential problems. For example—in case the parent constructor does something else other than just initializing properties, such as DOM manipulation, then while assigning a new instance of the parent constructor, to the `prototype` property, of the child constructor, can cause problems.

Therefore, the ES6 classes provide a better and easier way to inherit the existing constructors and classes. We will see more on this later in this chapter.

The constructors of primitive data types

The primitive data, types such as boolean, string, and number, have their constructor counterparts. These counterpart constructors behave like wrappers for these primitive types. For example, the `String` constructor is used to create a string object that contains an internal `[[PrimitiveValue]]` property that holds the actual primitive value.

At runtime, wherever necessary, the primitive values are wrapped with their constructor counterparts, and also the counterpart objects are treated as primitive values, so that the code works as expected. Consider this example code to understand how it works:

```
var s1 = "String";
var s2 = new String("String");

console.log(typeof s1);
console.log(typeof s2);

console.log(s1 == s2);
console.log(s1.length);
```

The output is as follows:

```
string
object
true
6
```

Here, `s1` is a primitive type, and `s2` is an object although applying the `==` operator on them gives us a `true` result. `s1` is a primitive type but still we are able to access the length property however primitive types shouldn't have any properties.

All this is happening because the previous code was converted into this on runtime:

```
var s1 = "String";
var s2 = new String("String");

console.log(typeof s1);
console.log(typeof s2);

console.log(s1 == s2.valueOf());
console.log((new String(s1)).length);
```

Here, we can see how the primitive value was wrapped with its constructor counterpart, and how the object counterpart was treated as primitive value when necessary. Therefore, the code works as expected.

The primitive types introduced from ES6 onwards won't allow their counterpart functions to be invoked as constructors, that is, we can't explicitly wrap them using their object counterparts. We saw this behavior while learning symbols.

The `null` and `undefined` primitive types don't have any counterpart constructors.

Using classes

We saw that JavaScript's object-oriented model is based on the constructors and prototype-based inheritance. Well, the ES6 classes are just new a syntax for the existing model. Classes do not introduce a new object-oriented model to JavaScript.

The ES6 classes aim to provide a much simpler and clearer syntax for dealing with the constructors and inheritance.

In fact, classes are functions. Classes are just a new syntax for creating functions that are used as constructors. Creating functions using the classes that aren't used as constructors doesn't make any sense, and offer no benefits. Rather, it makes your code difficult to read, as it becomes confusing. Therefore, use classes only if you want to use it for constructing objects. Let's have a look at classes in detail.

Defining a class

Just as there are two ways of defining functions, function declaration and function expression, there are two ways to define a class: using the class declaration and the class expression.

The class declaration

For defining a class using the class declaration, you need to use the `class` keyword, and a name for the class.

Here is a code example to demonstrate how to define a class using the class declaration:

```
class Student
{
  constructor(name)
  {
    this.name = name;
  }
}

var s1 = new Student("Eden");
console.log(s1.name); //Output "Eden"
```

Here, we created a class named `Student`. Then, we defined a `constructor` method in it. Finally, we created a new instance of the class—an object, and logged the `name` property of the object.

Walking You Through Classes

The body of a class is in the curly brackets, that is, { }. This is where we need to define methods. Methods are defined without the `function` keyword, and a comma is not used in between the methods.

Classes are treated as functions, and internally the class name is treated as the function name, and the body of the `constructor` method is treated as the body of the function.

There can only be one `constructor` method in a class. Defining more than one constructor will throw the `SyntaxError` exception.

All the code inside a class body is executed in the `strict` mode, by default.

The previous code is the same as this code when written using function:

```
function Student(name)
{
  this.name = name;
}

var s1 = new Student("Eden");
console.log(s1.name); //Output "Eden"
```

To prove that a class is a function, consider this code:

```
class Student
{
  constructor(name)
  {
    this.name = name;
  }
}


function School(name)
{
  this.name = name;
}

console.log(typeof Student);
console.log(typeof School == typeof Student);
```

The output is as follows:

```
function
true
```

Here, we can see that a class is a function. It's just a new syntax for creating a function.

The class expression

A class expression has a similar syntax to a class declaration. However, with class expressions, you are able to omit the class name. Class body and behavior remains the same in both the ways.

Here is a code example to demonstrate how to define a class using a class expression:

```
var Student = class {
  constructor(name)
  {
    this.name = name;
  }
}

var s1 = new Student("Eden");
console.log(s1.name); //Output "Eden"
```

Here, we stored a reference of the class in a variable, and used it to construct the objects.

The previous code is the same as this code when written using function:

```
var Student = function(name) {
  this.name = name;
}

var s1 = new Student("Eden");
console.log(s1.name); //Output "Eden"
```

The prototype methods

All the methods in the body of the class are added to the `prototype` property of the class. The `prototype` property is the prototype of the objects created using class.

Here is an example that shows how to add methods to the `prototype` property of a class:

```
class Person
{
  constructor(name, age)
  {
    this.name = name;
    this.age = age;
  }
```

[141]

```
    printProfile()
    {
      console.log("Name is: " + this.name + " and Age is: " + 
this.age);
    }
}

var p = new Person("Eden", 12)
p.printProfile();

console.log("printProfile" in p.__proto__);
console.log("printProfile" in Person.prototype);
```

The output is as follows:

```
Name is: Eden and Age is: 12
true
true
```

Here, we can see that the `printProfile` method was added to the `prototype` property of the class.

The previous code is the same as this code when written using function:

```
function Person(name, age)
{
  this.name = name;
  this.age = age;
}

Person.prototype.printProfile = function()
{
  console.log("Name is: " + this.name + " and Age is: " + 
this.age);
}

var p = new Person("Eden", 12)
p.printProfile();

console.log("printProfile" in p.__proto__);
console.log("printProfile" in Person.prototype);
```

The output is as follows:

```
Name is: Eden and Age is: 12
true
true
```

The get and set methods

In ES5, to add accessor properties to the objects, we had to use the `Object.defineProperty()` method. ES6 introduced the `get` and `set` prefixes for methods. These methods can be added to the object literals and classes for defining the `get` and `set` attributes of the accessor properties.

When `get` and `set` methods are used in a class body, they are added to the `prototype` property of the class.

Here is an example to demonstrate how to define the `get` and `set` methods in a class:

```
class Person
{
  constructor(name)
  {
    this._name_ = name;
  }

  get name(){
    return this._name_;
  }

  set name(name){
    this._name_ = name;
  }
}

var p = new Person("Eden");
console.log(p.name);
p.name = "John";
console.log(p.name);

console.log("name" in p.__proto__);
console.log("name" in Person.prototype);
console.log(Object.getOwnPropertyDescriptor(p.__proto__, "name").set);
console.log(Object.getOwnPropertyDescriptor(Person.prototype, "name").get);
console.log(Object.getOwnPropertyDescriptor(p, "_name_").value);
```

The output is as follows:

```
Eden
John
true
```

```
true
function name(name) { this._name_ = name; }
function name() { return this._name_; }
John
```

Here, we created an accessor property to encapsulate the _name_ property. We also logged some other information to prove that name is an accessor property, which is added to the prototype property of the class.

The generator method

To treat a concise method of an object literal as the generator method, or to treat a method of a class as the generator method, we can simply prefix it with the * character.

The generator method of a class is added to the prototype property of the class.

Here is an example to demonstrate how to define a generator method in class:

```
class myClass
{
  * generator_function()
  {
    yield 1;
    yield 2;
    yield 3;
    yield 4;
    yield 5;
  }

}

var obj = new myClass();

let generator = obj.generator_function();

console.log(generator.next().value);
console.log(generator.next().value);
console.log(generator.next().value);
console.log(generator.next().value);
console.log(generator.next().value);
console.log(generator.next().done);

console.log("generator_function" in myClass.prototype);
```

The output is as follows:

```
1
2
3
4
5
true
true
```

The static methods

The methods that are added to the body of the class with the `static` prefix are called as static methods. Static methods are the own methods of the class, that is, they are not added to the `prototype` property of the class, rather they are added to the class itself. For example, the `String.fromCharCode()` method is a static method of the `String` constructor, that is, `fromCharCode` is the own property of the `String` function itself.

Static methods are often used to create utility functions for an application.

Here is an example to demonstrate how to define and use a static method in class:

```
class Student
{
  constructor(name)
  {
    this.name = name;
  }

  static findName(student)
  {
    return student.name;
  }
}

var s = new Student("Eden");
var name = Student.findName(s);

console.log(name); //Output "Eden"
```

Here, `findName` is a static method of the `Student` class.

The previous code is the same as this code when written using function:

```
function Student(name)
{
    this.name = name;
}

Student.findName = function(student){
  return student.name;
}

var s = new Student("Eden");
var name = Student.findName(s);

console.log(name); //Output "Eden"
```

Implementing inheritance in classes

Earlier in this chapter, we saw how difficult it was to implement inheritance hierarchy in functions. Therefore, ES6 aims to make it easy by introducing the `extends` clause, and the `super` keyword for classes.

By using the `extends` clause, a class can inherit static and non-static properties of another constructor (which may or may not be defined using a class).

The `super` keyword is used in two ways:

- It's used in a class `constructor` method to call the parent constructor
- When used inside methods of a class, it references the static and non-static methods of the parent constructor

Here is an example to demonstrate how to implement the inheritance hierarchy in the constructors using the `extends` clause, and the `super` keyword:

```
function A(a)
{
  this.a = a;
}

A.prototype.printA = function(){
  console.log(this.a);
}
```

```
class B extends A
{
  constructor(a, b)
  {
    super(a);
    this.b = b;
  }

  printB()
  {
    console.log(this.b);
  }

  static sayHello()
  {
    console.log("Hello");
  }
}

class C extends B
{
  constructor(a, b, c)
  {
    super(a, b);
    this.c = c;
  }

  printC()
  {
    console.log(this.c);
  }

  printAll()
  {
    this.printC();
    super.printB();
    super.printA();
  }
}

var obj = new C(1, 2, 3);
obj.printAll();

C.sayHello();
```

The output is as follows:

```
3
2
1
Hello
```

Here, `A` is a function constructor; `B` is a class that inherits `A`; `C` is a class that inherits `B`; and as `B` inherits `A`, therefore `C` also inherits `A`.

As a class can inherit a function constructor, we can also inherit the prebuilt function constructors, such as `String` and `Array`, and also the custom function constructors using the classes instead of other *hacky* ways that we used to use.

The previous example also shows how and where to use the `super` keyword. Remember that inside the `constructor` method, you need to use `super` before using the `this` keyword. Otherwise, an exception is thrown.

> If a child class doesn't have a `constructor` method, then the default behavior will invoke the `constructor` method of the parent class.

The computed method names

You can also decide the name of the static and non-static methods of a class and concise methods of a object literal on runtime, that is, you can define the name of methods via expressions. Here is an example to demonstrate this:

```
class myClass
{
  static ["my" + "Method"](){
    console.log("Hello");
  }
}

myClass["my" + "Method"](); //Output "Hello"
```

The computed property names also allow you to use symbols as keys for the methods. Here is an example to demonstrate this:

```
var s = Symbol("Sample");

class myClass
{
  static [s]()
  {
    console.log("Hello");
  }
}

myClass[s](); //Output "Hello"
```

The attributes of properties

When using class, the attributes of the static and non-static properties of constructor are different than when declared using function:

- The static methods are writable and configurable, but not enumerable
- The `prototype` property and the `prototype.constructor` property of class is not writable, numerable, or configurable
- The properties of the `prototype` property are writable and configurable, but not enumerable

Classes are not hoisted!

You can call a function before its defined, that is, function calls can be made above the function definition. But in case of class, you cannot use a class before its defined. Trying to do so in classes will throw the `ReferenceError` exception.

Here is an example to demonstrate this:

```
myFunc();
function myFunc(){}

var obj = new myClass(); //throws ReferenceError exception
class myClass{}
```

Overriding the result of the constructor method

The `constructor` method, by default, returns the new instance if there is no `return` statement in it. If there is a `return` statement, then whatever is the value in the `return` statement is returned.

Here is an example to demonstrate this:

```
class myClass
{
  constructor()
  {
    return Object.create(null);
  }
}

console.log(new myClass() instanceof myClass); //Output "false"
```

The "Symbol.species" static accessor property

The `@@species` static accessor property is optionally added to a child constructor, in order to signal the methods of the parent constructor, about what the constructor should use if the parent constructor's methods are returning new instances. If the `@@species` static accessor property is not defined on a child constructor, then the methods of the parent constructor can use the default constructor.

Consider this example to understand the use of `@@species` — the `map()` method of the array objects returns a new `Array` instance. If we call the `map()` method of an object that inherits an array object, then the `map()` method returns a new instance of the child constructor instead of the `Array` constructor, which is not what we always want. Therefore, ES6 introduced the `@@species` property, which provides a way to signal such kind of functions, to use a different constructor instead of the default constructor.

Here is a code example to demonstrate how to use the `@@species` static accessor property:

```
class myCustomArray1 extends Array
{
   static get [Symbol.species]()
   {
     return Array;
   }
```

```
}

class myCustomArray2 extends Array{}

var arr1 = new myCustomArray1(0, 1, 2, 3, 4);
var arr2 = new myCustomArray2(0, 1, 2, 3, 4);

console.log(arr1 instanceof myCustomArray1);
console.log(arr2 instanceof myCustomArray2);

arr1 = arr1.map(function(value){ return value + 1; })
arr2 = arr2.map(function(value){ return value + 1; })

console.log(arr1 instanceof myCustomArray1);
console.log(arr2 instanceof myCustomArray2);

console.log(arr1 instanceof Array);
console.log(arr2 instanceof Array);
```

The output is as follows:

```
true
true
false
true
true
false
```

It is recommended that if you are creating a JavaScript library, then the methods of the constructors in your library should always look for the @@species property while returning new instances. Here is an example to demonstrate this:

```
//Assume myArray1 is part of library
class myArray1
{

  //default @@species. Child class will inherit this property
  static get [Symbol.species]()
  {
    //default constructor
    return this;
  }

  mapping()
  {
```

```
      return new this.constructor[Symbol.species]();
  }
}

class myArray2 extends myArray1
{
  static get [Symbol.species]()
  {
    return myArray1;
  }
}

var arr = new myArray2();

console.log(arr instanceof myArray2); //Output "true"

arr = arr.mapping();

console.log(arr instanceof myArray1); //Output "true"
```

In case you don't want to define a default @@species property in parent constructors, then you can use the if...else conditional to check whether the @@species property is defined or not. But the previous pattern is preferred. The built-in map() method also uses the previous pattern.

All the built-in methods of the JavaScript constructors in ES6 look for a @@species property if they return a new instance. For example, the methods of Array, Map, ArrayBuffer, Promise, and other such constructors look for the @@species property if they return new instances.

The "new.target" implicit parameter

ES6 adds a parameter named new.target to all the functions. The dot in between is a part of the parameter name.

The default value of new.target is undefined. But when a function is invoked as a constructor, the value of the new.target parameter depends on the following conditions:

- If a constructor is invoked using a new operator, then new.target points to this constructor
- If a constructor is invoked via super keyword, then the value of new.target in it is the same as the value of new.target of the constructor that is called super.

Inside an arrow function, the value of new.target is the same as the value of new.target of the surrounding non-arrow function.

Here is an example code to demonstrate this:

```
function myConstructor()
{
  console.log(new.target.name);
}

class myClass extends myConstructor
{
  constructor()
  {
    super();
  }
}

var obj1 = new myClass();
var obj2 = new myConstructor();
```

The output is as follows:

```
myClass
myConstructor
```

Using "super" in the object literals

The super keyword can also be used in the concise methods of the object literals. The super keyword in concise methods of the object literals, has the same value as the [[prototype]] property of the object defined by the object literal.

In the object literals, super is used to access the over-ridden properties by the child object.

Here is an example to demonstrate how to use super in object literals:

```
var obj1 = {
  print(){
    console.log("Hello");
  }
}

var obj2 = {
  print(){
```

```
        super.print();
    }
}

Object.setPrototypeOf(obj2, obj1);
obj2.print(); //Output "Hello"
```

Summary

In this chapter, we first learned the basics of the object-oriented programming using ES5. Then, we jumped into ES6 classes, and learned how it makes easy for us to read and write the object-oriented JavaScript code. We also learned miscellaneous features, such as the `new.target` and accessor methods.

In the next chapter, we will learn how to create and use the ES6 modules.

8
Modular Programming

Modular programming is one of the most important and frequently used software design techniques. Unfortunately, JavaScript didn't support modules natively that lead JavaScript programmers to use alternative techniques to achieve modular programming in JavaScript. But now, ES6 brings modules in to JavaScript officially.

This chapter is all about how to create and import JavaScript modules. In this chapter, we will first learn how the modules were created earlier, and then we will jump to the new built-in module system that was introduced in ES6, known as the ES6 modules.

In this chapter, we'll cover:

- What is modular programming?
- The benefits of modular programming
- The basics of IIFE modules, AMD, UMD, and CommonJS
- Creating and importing the ES6 modules
- The basics of the Modular Loader
- Creating a basic JavaScript library using modules

The JavaScript modules in a nutshell

The practice of breaking down programs and libraries into modules is called modular programming.

In JavaScript, a module is a collection of related objects, functions, and other components of a program or library that are wrapped together and isolated from the scope of the rest of the program or library.

A module exports some variables to the outside program to let it access the components wrapped by the module. To use a module, a program needs to import the module and the variables exported by the module.

A module can also be split into further modules called as its submodules, thus creating a module hierarchy.

Modular programming has many benefits. Some benefits are:

- It keeps our code both cleanly separated and organized by splitting into multiple modules
- Modular programming leads to fewer global variables, that is, it eliminates the problem of global variables, because modules don't interface via the global scope, and each module has its own scope
- Makes code reusability easier as importing and using the same modules in different projects is easier
- It allows many programmers to collaborate on the same program or library, by making each programmer to work on a particular module with a particular functionality
- Bugs in an application can easily be easily identified as they are localized to a particular module

Implementing modules – the old way

Before ES6, JavaScript had never supported modules natively. Developers used other techniques and third-party libraries to implement modules in JavaScript.

Using **Immediately-invoked function expression (IIFE)**, **Asynchronous Module Definition (AMD)**, **CommonJS**, and **Universal Module Definition (UMD)** are various popular ways of implementing modules in ES5. As these ways were not native to JavaScript, they had several problems. Let's see an overview of each of these old ways of implementing modules.

The Immediately-Invoked Function Expression

The IIFE is used to create an anonymous function that invokes itself. Creating modules using IIFE is the most popular way of creating modules.

Let's see an example of how to create a module using IIFE:

```
//Module Starts

(function(window){
  var sum = function(x, y){
    return x + y;
  }

  var sub = function(x, y){
    return x - y;
  }

  var math = {
    findSum: function(a, b){
      return sum(a,b);
    },
    findSub: function(a, b){
      return sub(a, b);
    }
  }

  window.math = math;
})(window)

//Module Ends

console.log(math.findSum(1, 2)); //Output "3"
console.log(math.findSub(1, 2)); //Output "-1"
```

Here, we created a module using IIFE. The `sum` and `sub` variables are global to the module, but not visible outside of the module. The `math` variable is exported by the module to the main program to expose the functionalities that it provides.

This module works completely independent of the program, and can be imported by any other program by simply copying it into the source code, or importing it as a separate file.

> A library using IIFE, such as jQuery, wraps its all of its APIs in a single IIFE module. When a program uses a jQuery library, it automatically imports the module.

Asynchronous Module Definition

AMD is a specification for implementing modules in browser. AMD is designed by keeping the browser limitations in mind, that is, it imports modules asynchronously to prevent blocking the loading of a webpage. As AMD is not a native browser specification, we need to use an AMD library. **RequireJS** is the most popular AMD library.

Let's see an example on how to create and import modules using RequireJS. According to the AMD specification, every module needs to be represented by a separate file. So first, create a file named math.js that represents a module. Here is the sample code that will be inside the module:

```
define(function(){
  var sum = function(x, y){
    return x + y;
  }
  var sub = function(x, y){
    return x - y;
  }
  var math = {
    findSum: function(a, b){
      return sum(a,b);
    },
    findSub: function(a, b){
      return sub(a, b);
    }
  }
  return math;
});
```

Here, the module exports the math variable to expose its functionality.

Now, let's create a file named index.js, which acts like the main program that imports the module and the exported variables. Here is the code that will be inside the index.js file:

```
require(["math"], function(math){
  console.log(math.findSum(1, 2)); //Output "3"
  console.log(math.findSub(1, 2)); //Output "-1"
})
```

Here, math variable in the first parameter is the name of the file that is treated as the AMD module. The .js extension to the file name is added automatically by RequireJS.

The math variable, which is in the second parameter, references the exported variable.

Here, the module is imported asynchronously, and the callback is also executed asynchronously.

CommonJS

CommonJS is a specification for implementing modules in **Node.js**. According to the CommonJS specification, every module needs to be represented by a separate file. The CommonJS modules are imported synchronously.

Let's see an example on how to create and import modules using CommonJS. First, we will create a file named math.js that represents a module. Here is a sample code that will be inside the module:

```
var sum = function(x, y){
   return x + y;
}

var sub = function(x, y){
   return x - y;
}

var math = {
   findSum: function(a, b){
      return sum(a,b);
   },

   findSub: function(a, b){
      return sub(a, b);
   }
}

exports.math = math;
```

Here, the module exports the math variable to expose its functionality.

Now, let's create a file named index.js, which acts like the main program that imports the module. Here is the code that will be inside the index.js file:

```
var math = require("./math").math;

console.log(math.findSum(1, 2)); //Output "3"
console.log(math.findSub(1, 2)); //Output "-1"
```

Here, the math variable is the name of the file that is treated as module. The .js extension to the file name is added automatically by CommonJS.

Modular Programming

Universal Module Definition

We saw three different specifications of implementing modules. These three specifications have their own respective ways of creating and importing modules. Wouldn't it have been great if we can create modules that can be imported as an IIFE, AMD, or CommonJS module?

UMD is a set of techniques that is used to create modules that can be imported as an IIFE, CommonJS, or AMD module. Therefore now, a program can import third-party modules, irrespective of what module specification it is using.

The most popular UMD technique is `returnExports`. According to the `returnExports` technique, every module needs to be represented by a separate file. So, let's create a file named `math.js` that represents a module. Here is the sample code that will be inside the module:

```javascript
(function (root, factory) {
  //Environment Detection
  if (typeof define === 'function' && define.amd) {
    define([], factory);
  } else if (typeof exports === 'object') {
    module.exports = factory();
  } else {
    root.returnExports = factory();
  }
}(this, function () {
  //Module Definition
  var sum = function(x, y){
    return x + y;
  }
  var sub = function(x, y){
    return x - y;
  }
  var math = {
    findSum: function(a, b){
      return sum(a,b);
    },
    findSub: function(a, b){
      return sub(a, b);
    }
  }
  return math;
}));
```

Now, you can successfully import the `math.js` module any way that you wish, for instance, by using CommonJS, RequireJS, or IIFE.

Implementing modules – the new way

ES6 introduced a new module system called ES6 modules. The ES6 modules are supported natively and therefore, they can be referred as the standard JavaScript modules.

You should consider using ES6 modules instead of the old ways, because they have neater syntax, better performance, and many new APIs that are likely to be packed as the ES6 modules.

Let's have a look at the ES6 modules in detail.

Creating the ES6 modules

Every ES6 module needs to be represented by a separate .js file. An ES6 module can contain any JavaScript code, and it can export any number of variables.

A module can export a variable, function, class, or any other entity.

We need to use the `export` statement in a module to export variables. The `export` statement comes in many different formats. Here are the formats:

```
export {variableName};
export {variableName1, variableName2, variableName3};
export {variableName as myVariableName};
export {variableName1 as myVariableName1, variableName2 as myVariableName2};
export {variableName as default};
export {variableName as default, variableName1 as myVariableName1, variableName2};
export default function(){};
export {variableName1, variableName2} from "myAnotherModule";
export * from "myAnotherModule";
```

Here are the differences in these formats:

- The first format exports a variable.
- The second format is used to export multiple variables.
- The third format is used to export a variable with another name, that is, an alias.
- The fourth format is used to export multiple variables with different names.
- The fifth format uses `default` as the alias. We will find out the use of this later in this chapter.

Modular Programming

- The sixth format is similar to fourth format, but it also has the `default` alias.
- The seventh format works similar to fifth format, but here you can place an expression instead of a variable name.
- The eighth format is used to export the exported variables of a submodule.
- The ninth format is used to export all the exported variables of a submodule.

Here are some important things that you need to know about the `export` statement:

- An export statement can be used anywhere in a module. It's not compulsory to use it at the end of the module.
- There can be any number of `export` statements in a module.
- You cannot export variables on demand. For example, placing the `export` statement in the `if...else` condition throws an error. Therefore, we can say that the module structure needs to be static, that is, exports can be determined on compile time.
- You cannot export the same variable name or alias multiple times. But you can export a variable multiple times with a different alias.
- All the code inside a module is executed in the `strict` mode by default.
- The values of the exported variables can be changed inside the module that exported them.

Importing the ES6 modules

To import a module, we need to use the `import` statement. The `import` statement comes in many different formats. Here are the formats:

```
import x from "module-relative-path";
import {x} from "module-relative-path";
import {x1 as x2} from "module-relative-path";
import {x1, x2} from "module-relative-path";
import {x1, x2 as x3} from "module-relative-path";
import x, {x1, x2} from "module-relative-path";
import "module-relative-path";
import * as x from "module-relative-path";
import x1, * as x2 from "module-relative-path";
```

An `import` statement consists of two parts: the variable names we want to import and the relative path of the module.

Here are the differences in these formats:

- In the first format, the `default` alias is imported. The x is alias of the `default` alias.
- In the second format, the x variable is imported.
- The third format is the same as the second format. It's just that x2 is an alias of x1.
- In the fourth format, we import the x1 and x2 variables.
- In the fifth format, we import the x1 and x2 variables. The x3 is an alias of the x2 variable.
- In the sixth format, we import the x1 and x2 variable, and the `default` alias. The x is an alias of the `default` alias.
- In the seventh format, we just import the module. We do not import any of the variables exported by the module.
- In the eighth format, we import all the variables, and wrap them in an object called x. Even the `default` alias is imported.
- The ninth format is the same as the eighth format. Here, we give another alias to the `default` alias.

Here are some important things that you need to know about the `import` statement:

- While importing a variable, if we import it with an alias, then to refer to that variable, we have to use the alias and not the actual variable name, that is, the actual variable name will not be visible, only the alias will be visible.
- The `import` statement doesn't import a copy of the exported variables; rather, it makes the variables available in the scope of the program that imports it. Therefore, if you make a change to an exported variable inside the module, then the change is visible to the program that imports it.
- The imported variables are read-only, that is, you cannot reassign them to something else outside of the scope of the module that exports them.
- A module can only be imported once in a single instance of a JavaScript engine. If we try to import it again, then the already imported instance of the module will be used.
- We cannot import modules on demand. For example, placing the `import` statement in the `if...else` condition throws an error. Therefore, we can say that the imports should be able to be determined on compile time.

- The ES6 imports are faster than the AMD and CommonJS imports, because the ES6 imports are supported natively and also as importing modules and exporting variables are not decided on demand. Therefore, it makes JavaScript engine easier to optimize performance.

The module loader

A module loader is a component of a JavaScript engine that is responsible for importing modules.

The `import` statement uses the build-in module loader to import modules.

The built-in module loaders of the different JavaScript environments use different module loading mechanisms. For example, when we import a module in JavaScript running in the browsers, then the module is loaded from the server. On the other hand, when we import a module in Node.js, then the module is loaded from filesystem.

The module loader loads modules in a different manner, in different environments, to optimize the performance. For example, in the browsers, the module loader loads and executes modules asynchronously in order to prevent the importing of the modules that block the loading of a webpage.

You can programmatically interact with the built-in module loader using the module loader API to customize its behavior, intercept module loading, and fetch the modules on demand.

We can also use this API to create our own custom module loaders.

The specifications of the module loader are not specified in ES6. It is a separate standard, controlled by the **WHATWG** browser standard group. You can find the specifications of the module loader at http://whatwg.github.io/loader/.

The ES6 specifications only specify the `import` and `export` statements.

Using modules in browsers

The code inside the `<script>` tag doesn't support the `import` statement, because the tag's synchronous nature is incompatible with the asynchronicity of the modules in browsers. Instead, you need to use the new `<module>` tag to import modules.

Using the new `<module>` tag, we can define a script as a module. Now, this module can import other modules using the `import` statement.

If you want to import a module using the `<script>` tag, then you have to use the **Module Loader API**.

The specifications of the `<module>` tag are not specified in ES6.

Using modules in the eval() function

You cannot use the `import` and `export` statements in the `eval()` function. To import modules in the `eval()` function, you need to use the Module Loader API.

The default exports vs. the named exports

When we export a variable with the `default` alias, then it's called as a **default export**. Obviously, there can only be one default export in a module, as an alias can be used only once.

All the other exports except the default export are called as **named exports**.

It's recommended that a module should either use default export or named exports. It's not a good practice to use both together.

The default export is used when we want to export only one variable. On the other hand, the named exports are used when we want to export the multiple variables.

Diving into an example

Let's create a basic JavaScript library using the ES6 modules. This will help us understand how to use the `import` and `export` statements. We will also learn how a module can import other modules.

The library that we will create is going to be a math library, which provides basic logarithmic and trigonometric functions. Let's get started with creating our library:

- Create a file named `math.js`, and a directory named `math_modules`. Inside the `math_modules` directory, create two files named `logarithm.js` and `trigonometry.js`, respectively.

    Here, the `math.js` file is the root module, whereas the `logarithm.js` and the `trigonometry.js` files are its submodules.

- Place this code inside the `logarithm.js` file:

    ```
    var LN2 = Math.LN2;
    var N10 = Math.LN10;
    ```

Modular Programming

```javascript
function getLN2()
{
  return LN2;
}

function getLN10()
{
  return LN10;
}

export {getLN2, getLN10};
```

Here, the module is exporting the functions named as exports.

It's preferred that the low-level modules in a module hierarchy should export all the variables separately, because it may be possible that a program may need just one exported variable of a library. In this case, a program can import this module and a particular function directly. Loading all the modules when you need just one module is a bad idea in terms of performance.

Similarly, place this code in the `trigonometry.js` file:

```javascript
var cos = Math.cos;
var sin = Math.sin;

function getSin(value)
{
  return sin(value);
}

function getCos(value)
{
  return cos(value);
}

export {getCos, getSin};
```

Here we do something similar. Place this code inside the `math.js` file, which acts as the root module:

```javascript
import * as logarithm from "math_modules/logarithm";
import * as trigonometry from "math_modules/trigonometry";

export default {
  logarithm: logarithm,
  trigonometry: trigonometry
}
```

It doesn't contain any library functions. Instead, it makes easy for a program to import the complete library. It imports its submodules, and then exports their exported variables to the main program.

Here, in case the `logarithm.js` and `trigonometry.js` scripts depends on other submodules, then the `math.js` module shouldn't import those submodules, because `logarithm.js` and `trigonometry.js` are already importing them.

Here is the code using which a program can import the complete library:

```
import math from "math";

console.log(math.trigonometry.getSin(3));
console.log(math.logarithm.getLN2(3));
```

Summary

In this chapter, we saw what modular programming is and learned different modular programming specifications. Finally, we created a basic library using the modular programming design technique. Now, you should be confident enough to build the JavaScript apps using the ES6 modules.

Index

A

AJAX requests 76
apply() method 10
apply(target, thisValue, arguments) method 127
array buffers 49
array destructuring assignment
  about 14
  default values, for variables 16
  nested array destructuring 17
  rest operator, using 15, 16
  using, as parameter 17
  values, ignoring 15
arrays
  about 44
  Array.from() method 44
  Array.of()method 44, 45
  copyWithin() method 47
  entries() method 48
  fill() method 45
  findIndex() method 47
  find() method 46
  keys() method 48
  values() method 48
arrow functions
  about 19
  differentiating, with traditional functions 22
  this value 20, 21
asynchronous code
  writing 76
asynchronous code, involving callbacks 80-82
asynchronous code, involving events 77-79

Asynchronous Module Definition (AMD)
  about 156
  used, for implementing modules 158
attributes, of properties 149

B

base object 134
Battery Status API 75, 97
binary notation 26
browsers
  modules, using in 164

C

child object 134
class declaration 139, 140
classes
  defining 139
  inheritance, implementing in 146-148
  static methods, using in 145, 146
  using 139
class expression 141
codePointAt() method 36
code unit 35
collections
  about 49
  array buffers 49, 50
  Map 54
  Set 52, 53
  typed arrays 51, 52
  WeakMap 55
  WeakSet 53
CommonJS
  about 156
  used, for implementing modules 159

computed method names 148
const keyword
  about 6
  constant variables, scope 7
  objects using constant variables,
    referencing 7
constructor method
  result, overriding of 150
constructors, of primitive data
    types 137, 138
construct(target, arguments) method 128
copyWithin() method 47

D

data type 132
default exports
  versus named exports 165
default parameter values 8
defineProperty(target, property, descriptor)
    method
  about 123
  rules 124
deleteProperty(target, property) method
  about 124
  rules 124
derived object 134
descriptor object, accessor property
  configurable property 105
  enumerable property 105
  get function 105
  set function 105
descriptor object, data property
  configurable property 104
  enumerable property 104
  value property 104
  writable property 104
destructuring assignment
  about 14
  array destructuring assignment 14
  object destructuring assignment 18

E

endsWith() function 38
enhanced object literals
  about 22
  computed property names 23
  methods, defining 23
  properties, defining 22
entries() method 48
enumerate(target) method
  about 124
  rules 125
ES5 25
ES6
  about 25
  const keyword 6
  let keyword 1
ES6 modules
  about 155
  creating 161, 162
  example 165-167
  importing 162, 163
ES6 symbols
  about 59, 60
  new operator 60
  Object.getOwnPropertySymbols()
    method 62
  Symbol.for(string) method 62
  typeof operator 60
  using, as property keys 61
eval() function
  modules, using in 165
executor 83
expressions
  about 41, 42
  multiline strings 42, 43
  raw strings 43

F

fill() method 45
findIndex() method 47
find() method 46
floating-point arithmetic
  URL 31
for...of loop 71
functions
  for storing numbers 50

G

generator method 144, 145
generators
  about 66, 67

for...of keyword 71
return(value) method 68
throw(exception) method 69, 70
yield* keyword 70
get method 143, 144
getOwnPropertyDescriptor(target, property) method
  about 122
  rules 123
getPrototypeOf(target) method
  about 120
  rules 120
get(target, property, receiver) method
  about 115, 116
  rules 117

H

handler 114
has(target, property) method
  about 118
  rules 119
HTML5 75

I

Immediately-invoked function expression (IIFE)
  about 156
  used, for implementing modules 156, 157
includes() method 37
inheritance
  about 133
  example 134-136
  implementing, in classes 146-148
isExtensible(target) method
  about 119
  rules 120
isFinite() function 29
isNaN() function 28
iteration protocols
  about 64
  iterable protocol 65
  iterator protocol 64

J

JavaScript
  objects, creating in 132, 133
JavaScript APIs, based on Promises
  about 97
  Battery Status API 97
  Web Cryptography API 98, 99
JavaScript data types
  about 132
  Boolean 132
  null 132
  number 132
  object 132
  string 132
  symbol 132
  undefined 132
JavaScript execution model 76
JavaScript modules 155
JavaScript objects 25
jQuery 76

K

keys() method 48

L

let keyword
  about 1
  block scoped variables, declaring 3
  function scoped variables, declaring 2
  variables, re-declaring 4, 5

M

Map 54
Math
  about 31
  arithmetic related operations 32
  trigonometry related operations 32
miscellaneous methods
  about 33
  Math.clz32() function 33
  Math.imul() function 33
  Math.sign() function 34
  Math.trunc() function 34

modular programming
  about 155
  benefits 156
Module Loader API 165
modules
  implementing 156, 161
  implementing, Asynchronous Module
      Definition (AMD) used 158
  implementing, CommonJS used 159
  implementing, Immediately-invoked
      function expression (IIFE)
      used 156, 157
  implementing, Universal Module
      Definition (UMD) used 160
  using, in browsers 164
  using, in eval() function 165

N

named exports
  versus default exports 165
new operator 60
new.target implicit parameter 152
Node.js 159
non-tail calls
  converting, into tail calls 73, 74
normalization
  about 38
  case study 38-40
  URL 40
Number.EPSILON property 30
numbers
  binary notation 26
  Number.isFinite() method 29
  Number.isInteger() method 27
  Number.isNaN() method 28
  Number.isNaN()method 29
  Number.isSafeInteger() method 30
  octal notation 26
  working with 25

O

object
  __proto__ property 56
  about 56
  creating, in JavaScript 132, 133
  Object.assign() method 57, 58
  Object.is() method 56
  Object.setPrototypeOf() method 57
object destructuring assignment
  about 17
  computed property names, destructing 19
  default values, for variables 18
  nested objects, destructing 19
  using, as parameter 19
Object.getOwnPropertySymbols()
      method 62
object literals
  super keyword, using in 153
object-oriented JavaScript
  about 131
  JavaScript data types 132
octal notation 26
ownKeys(target) method
  about 125, 126
  rules 127

P

parent object 134
Perl 14
preventExtensions(target) method
  about 121
  rules 122
primitive data types
  about 132
  constructors 137, 138
Promise pattern
  about 82
  catch(onRejected) method 91-93
  fulfillment value 84, 85
  Promise.all(iterable) method 95
  Promise constructor 83, 84
  Promise.race(iterable) method 96
  Promise.reject(value) method 94
  Promise.resolve(value) method 94
  states 84
  then(onFulfilled, onRejected) method 85-91
properties
  attributes 149
property keys
  ES6 symbols, using as 61

prototype methods
  about 141, 142
  generator 144, 145
  get 143
  set 143
proxies
  about 113
  use cases 129
Proxy API 114
Proxy.revocable(target, handler) method
  about 128
  use case 129
Python 35

R

Reflect API 101
Reflect object
  about 101
  Reflect.apply(function, this, args)
      method 102
  Reflect.construct(constructor, args,
      prototype) method 102, 103
  Reflect.defineProperty(object, property,
      descriptor) method 103, 104
  Reflect.deleteProperty(object, property)
      method 106
  Reflect.enumerate(object) method 107
  Reflect.get(object, property, this)
      method 107
  Reflect.getOwnPropertyDescriptor(object,
      property) method 109
  Reflect.getPrototypeOf(object)
      method 109, 110
  Reflect.has(object, property)
      method 110, 111
  Reflect.ownKeys(object) method 112
  Reflect.preventExtensions(object)
      method 111
  Reflect.set(object, property, value, this)
      method 108
  Reflect.setPrototypeOf(object, prototype)
      method 110
repeat() method 37
RequireJS 158
rest operator 16
rest parameter 13

return(value) method 68
Ruby 35

S

Set
  about 52, 53
  differentiating, with WeakSet 53
  unique values 52
set method 143, 144
setPrototypeOf(target, prototype) method
  about 120
  rules 121
set(target, property, value, receiver) method
  about 118
  rules 118
spread operator
  about 9, 10
  array values, merging with another
      array 11
  array values, pushing to another
      array 11, 12
  multiple arrays, spreading 12
  uses 11
states, Promise pattern
  fulfilled 84
  pending 84
  rejected 84
  settled 84
static methods
  using, in classes 145, 146
String.fromCodePoint() method 36
strings
  codePointAt() method 36
  endsWith() function 38
  expressions 40
  includes() method 37
  larger code points, escaping 36
  normalization 38
  repeat() method 37
  startsWith() method 37
  String.fromCodePoint() method 36
  template strings 40
  working with 35
subobject 134
super keyword
  using, in object literals 153

superobject 134
Symbol.for(string) method 62
Symbol() function 60
Symbol.species static accessor property 150-152

T

tag function 41
tagged template string 41
tail call optimization 72
tail calls
  about 72
  non-tail calls, converting into 73, 74
tail-recursion 72
target 114
target constructor 102
terminologies, proxies
  handler 114
  target 114
  traps 114
throw(exception) method 69, 70
traps
  about 114, 115
  apply(target, thisValue, arguments) method 127
  construct(target, arguments) method 128
  defineProperty(target, property, descriptor) method 123, 124
  deleteProperty(target, property) method 124
  enumerate(target) method 124
  getOwnPropertyDescriptor(target, property) method 122, 123
  getPrototypeOf(target) method 120
  get(target, property, receiver) method 115-117
  has(target, property) method 118, 119
  isExtensible(target) method 119
  ownKeys(target) method 125, 126
  preventExtensions(target) method 121, 122
  setPrototypeOf(target, prototype) method 120
  set(target, property, value, receiver) method 118

typed arrays
  about 51, 52
  constructors 51
typeof operator 60

U

Unicode string normalization
  URL 40
Universal Module Definition (UMD)
  about 156
  used, for implementing modules 160
UTF-8 35
UTF-16 35

V

values() method 48

W

WeakMap 55
WeakSet
  differentiating, with Set 53
Web Cryptography API 75, 98, 99
web workers 76
well-known symbols 63
WHATWG
  URL 164

Y

yield* keyword 70

Thank you for buying
Learning ECMAScript 6

About Packt Publishing

Packt, pronounced 'packed', published its first book, *Mastering phpMyAdmin for Effective MySQL Management*, in April 2004, and subsequently continued to specialize in publishing highly focused books on specific technologies and solutions.

Our books and publications share the experiences of your fellow IT professionals in adapting and customizing today's systems, applications, and frameworks. Our solution-based books give you the knowledge and power to customize the software and technologies you're using to get the job done. Packt books are more specific and less general than the IT books you have seen in the past. Our unique business model allows us to bring you more focused information, giving you more of what you need to know, and less of what you don't.

Packt is a modern yet unique publishing company that focuses on producing quality, cutting-edge books for communities of developers, administrators, and newbies alike. For more information, please visit our website at www.packtpub.com.

About Packt Open Source

In 2010, Packt launched two new brands, Packt Open Source and Packt Enterprise, in order to continue its focus on specialization. This book is part of the Packt Open Source brand, home to books published on software built around open source licenses, and offering information to anybody from advanced developers to budding web designers. The Open Source brand also runs Packt's Open Source Royalty Scheme, by which Packt gives a royalty to each open source project about whose software a book is sold.

Writing for Packt

We welcome all inquiries from people who are interested in authoring. Book proposals should be sent to author@packtpub.com. If your book idea is still at an early stage and you would like to discuss it first before writing a formal book proposal, then please contact us; one of our commissioning editors will get in touch with you.

We're not just looking for published authors; if you have strong technical skills but no writing experience, our experienced editors can help you develop a writing career, or simply get some additional reward for your expertise.

Rapid Underscore.js [Video]

ISBN: 978-1-78439-162-1 Duration: 00:49 hours

Harness the power of the extensive range of functionalities that come with Underscore.js

1. Take functional programming to the next level with the aid of the Underscore library.
2. Learn why Underscore is a great addition to any JavaScript programmer's toolbelt.
3. Create an exciting International Space Station project, one step at a time.

JavaScript Promises Essentials

ISBN: 978-1-78398-564-7 Paperback: 90 pages

Build fully functional web applications using Promises, the new standard in JavaScript

1. Integrate JavaScript Promises into your application by mastering the key concepts of the Promises API.
2. Replace complex nested callbacks in JavaScript with the more intuitive chained Promises.
3. Acquire the knowledge needed to start working with JavaScript Promises immediately.

Please check www.PacktPub.com for information on our titles

Mastering JavaScript Design Patterns

ISBN: 978-1-78398-798-6   Paperback: 290 pages

Discover how to use JavaScript design patterns to create powerful applications with reliable and maintainable code

1. Learn how to use tried and true software design methodologies to enhance your Javascript code.
2. Discover robust JavaScript implementations of classic as well as advanced design patterns.
3. Packed with easy-to-follow examples that can be used to create reusable code and extensible designs.

Introducing Grunt: The JavaScript Task Runner [Video]

ISBN: 978-1-78439-617-6   Duration: 01:00 hours

Speed up and streamline web development by automating workflows with Grunt

1. Automate your workflows to decrease the amount of time spent on menial tasks.
2. Cut out time-consuming extra steps and make it easy for everyone to share the same workflow tools.
3. Combine all the tasks used in the course to create a concise and compact deployment package.

Please check www.PacktPub.com for information on our titles

Printed in Great Britain
by Amazon